DEFIANCE AND DEVOTION

SELECTED CHASSIDIC DISCOURSES
DATING FROM THE ARREST AND LIBERATION
OF THE SIXTH LUBAVITCHER REBBE
RABBI YOSEF YITZCHAK SCHNEERSOHN נ״ע
IN 1927

בס"ד

Defiance and Devotion

**Selected Chassidic Discourses
Dating from the Arrest and Liberation
of the Sixth Lubavitcher Rebbe
Rabbi Yosef Yitzchak Schneersohn נ"ע
in 1927**

Translated by Rabbi Eliyahu Touger
Edited by Uri Kaploun

Kehot Publication Society
770 Eastern Parkway
Brooklyn, New York 11213

5756 · 1996

DEFIANCE AND DEVOTION

Published & Copyright © 1996
Kehot Publication Society
770 Eastern Parkway • Brooklyn, New York 11213
(718) 774-4000 • (718) 778-5436

All rights reserved. No part of this publication may be reproduced in any form or by any means, including photo-copying, without permission in writing from the copyright holder or the publisher.

ISBN 0-8266-0537-0

TABLE OF CONTENTS

Publisher's Foreword vii

Maamar
VeKibeil HaYehudim
וקבל היהודים את אשר החלו לעשות 1

Maamar
Yehi Havayah Elokeinu Imanu
יהי הוי-ה אלקינו עמנו, כאשר הי-ה עם אבותינו 53

Maamar
Havayah Li BeOzrai
הוי-ה לי בעוזרי, ואני אראה בשונאי 57

Maamar
Baruch HaGomel
ברוך... הגומל לחייבים טובות שגמלני טוב 85

Maamar
Asarah SheYoshvim
עשרה שיושבים ועוסקים בתורה, שכינה שרוי-ה ביניהם 95

Publisher's Foreword

In 1927, after incitement by the Yevsektzia, the virulently anti-religious Jewish Section of the Soviet Communist Party, the sixth Rebbe of Lubavitch, the saintly Rabbi Yosef Yitzchak Schneersohn נ״ע,[1] was incarcerated under capital arrest in Leningrad, interrogated, tortured and exiled, until ultimately — and miraculously — he was liberated. The five discourses in this volume all date from this period,[2] surely one of the most agonizing and turbulent epochs in all of our turbulent and agonizing history.

A superficial historian might thus be tempted to conclude that this noble epoch of literal self-sacrifice for the rescue of Jewry's threatened soul *gave rise to* these discourses. They appear so obviously to have sprouted out of the spiritual soil of those times. The opposite, though, is even truer: these discourses *gave rise to* this noble epoch, this time of literal self-sacrifice for the rescue of Jewry's threatened soul.

What is the potent message in these (and many other) *maamarim* that empowered them to deflect the natural course of Jewish history?

Above all, they embodied an explicit and fearless call to defy the Soviet regime, even at the cost of life itself. A dramatic example of this is the very first *maamar* in this volume.[3] When the author's successor, the seventh Rebbe of Lubavitch, Rabbi Menachem M. Schneerson,[4] republished it in 1951, he chose to append a contemporary document — a letter in which a certain rabbi records a factual and artless description of those

---

1. Known as the Rebbe Rayatz (an acronym of the Hebrew letters of his name).
2. The chronological connections between these discourses and his arrest on 15 Sivan, his reprieve from imprisonment and from capital sentence on *Gimmel Tammuz*, and his release from exile on *Yud-Beis-Yud-Gimmel* Tammuz, are explained in the respective paragraphs which orient the reader before each of the five *maamarim*.
3. The circumstances surrounding its delivery are described on p. 2 below.
4. Referred to throughout the present work as "the Rebbe."

days by one of the many stalwart communal functionaries who continued to serve their flock against all odds.[5]

This communal leader, who was not a chassid, relates how one Sunday in 1927 the GPU (formerly called the NKVD) interrogated him so insistently about the current movements of the Rebbe Rayatz that he immediately begged one of the elder chassidim to urge the Rebbe Rayatz to leave the city that very night. Little wonder, therefore, that on the following Wednesday evening, which was Purim Katan, as he was walking down Moscow's Archipova Street, he was stunned to discover that the Lubavitcher *shul* was brightly lit up. Hundreds of chassidim crowded its porch and staircase — even though every man there clearly knew that the presence there of the Rebbe Rayatz and his own attendance there endangered the lives of them all. Curious, the passerby entered and heard the "counter-revolutionary" message of the Rebbe Rayatz, loud and clear: Purim's battle of the spirit, in which the brute force of an anti-Semitic despot was vanquished by the pure breath of little children who were taught Torah by self-sacrificing teachers, is repeated in every generation.... The admiring listener's amazement was soon cut short. Observing a number of overly-attentive individuals who appeared to be spies of the GPU, he quickly left. And indeed, exactly four months later, the Rebbe Rayatz himself, together with many of those present, was arrested.

Not that imprisonment was a novel experience for him. He had already tasted the first of his seven prison terms when he was nine years old, but none was as excruciating as the incarceration of 1927. Though he found it more difficult to demand self-sacrifice of others than of himself, at a *farbrengen* a few years earlier he had once asked for a core team of faithful helpers who would undertake — at all costs — to organize *shiurim* for adults, establish underground *chadarim* for children, maintain a valid *mikveh* wherever they found themselves, and so on. In response, nine of these key volunteer activists

---

5. *Sefer HaMaamarim 5687-5688 [1927-1928],* p. 288ff.

met secretly soon after in Moscow, and entered into a covenant with him that they would pursue their tasks "until the last drop of blood."

* * *

In 1920, with the passing of his father, the fifth Rebbe of Lubavitch, Rabbi Sholom Ber Schneersohn,[6] the 39-year-old Rabbi Yosef Yitzchak had found himself thrown into the leadership of the *Chabad* chassidic community. In the wake of World War I, the Revolution of 1917, and the anarchy and pillage of the battles between Denikin's Cossacks and the new Red Army, the Russia that confronted him was impoverished and seething with religious persecution.

Painful as it is to record, the fact is that his most relentless enemy was the above-mentioned Yevsektzia, the Jewish Section of the Soviet Communist Party. In a frenzy of loyalty to the Party, its members exploited their linguistic and personal connections to serve as spies and informers. (In one town, for example, a young man flaunted his zeal by reporting his venerable father's activity in maintaining the local *mikveh*. His superiors duly rewarded him by charging him with the task of personally wresting its key from his hands.) The members of the Yevsektzia monitored the mail and the movements of their townsmen, and staged public trials of underground teachers which led to exile and torture in Siberian labor camps. Institutions were also put on trial: the first *cheder* to be tried and closed was that of Vitebsk, and the first *yeshivah* to be tried and closed was that of Rostov. And, true to the Bolshevik tradition, the verdicts were commonly written before the trials began.

Lacking the advantage of historical hindsight, the self-hating Jews of the Yevsektzia can hardly be blamed for their shortsightedness: they could hardly be expected to know that every single one of them was eventually going to be charged with treachery to the cause of the Revolution, and unceremoniously liquidated in Stalin's purges.

* * *

---

6. Known as the Rebbe Rashab (an acronym of the Hebrew letters of his name).

The fearless stand of the Rebbe Rayatz bore fruit in thousands of times and places. Probably every reader of these lines has listened in amazement to incredible first-person accounts of courage in the face of this brutal religious suppression. For years on end, one well-known *mashpia* declined opportunities to be released from imprisonment until he had managed to fabricate documents (a capital offense!) that would spirit every possible fellow Jew out of the USSR. The learned author of the gulag memoirs entitled *Subbota,* which means "the Sabbath-observer," lived a life of self-sacrifice that cost him 20 years in Siberia. At the other end of the country, in Russian Georgia, a young chassidic woman lay down on the street in front of a bulldozer that was storming its way towards the local *shul* — and lived to tell the tale.[7] Many other chassidim, too — some whose date and place of burial are known to no man, some who have passed on from this world, and some who are eagerly awaiting the coming of *Mashiach* — risked their lives in order to observe a single *mitzvah,* or in order to save the life of a single stranger. One of the last survivors of that unique generation of self-effacing and self-sacrificing giants of the spirit was the diminutive Reb Abba Pliskin, of sainted memory. After dodging the NKVD for decades and finally leaving the USSR, this noiseless lamplighter introduced many of the Australian and American readers of the present work to the riches of *Chassidus.*

* * *

---

7. One of the few humorous episodes of those days took place in the same province. In the early 1920s, a confident young Lubavitcher chassid toured its Jewish communities, reading out those clauses of the revolutionary constitution which (at least nominally) permitted religious activity. As part of his spiel, which was aimed at encouraging the local people to dare to re-establish their destroyed synagogues and *mikvaos,* he generously praised the Communist authorities for their religious tolerance. He must have done this very convincingly — because one of his listeners, a member of the Ispolcom (the officially-appointed municipal council), mistook him for a representative of the central government! Deeply impressed, he promised there and then to pay for the reconstruction of the local *mikveh,* and he kept his promise.

In recent years, this extraordinary epoch has been increasingly documented by a flood of memoirs, interviews, and systematic historical accounts, both popular and scholarly.[8] Above all, the Rebbe Rayatz's own account of his arrest and liberation is told in *Reshimas HaMaasar,* which is due to appear in Vol. IV of the English translation of his classic *Likkutei Dibburim.* Reading this document gives one an inkling of how the chassidic teachings — and the daily example — of the Rebbe Rayatz actually *gave rise to* a unique epoch in Jewish history.

* * *

The Rebbe Rayatz once referred to the anniversary of his liberation as *moed hamoadim* — "the festival of festivals."[9] The Rebbe explained this as follows:[10] "A festival marks the day on which a miracle was performed. *Yud-Beis* Tammuz marks a time and a miracle of general concern — a miracle involving the head of the Jewish people, a festival from which derive all particular festivals and miracles."

---

8. Among those available in English (and this is a very partial list): a powerful and readable forthcoming book by Rabbi Dr. Alter Ben Zion Metzger entitled *The Heroic Struggle* (on the arrest, imprisonment and liberation of the Rebbe Rayatz); a documented article by Dr. William W. Brickman entitled "Unyielding Yiddishkeit: The Jewish Response to the Communist Campaign against the Jewish Religion in the Soviet Union, 1917-1938," with an appended list of historical sources, in *The Uforatzto Journal,* Spring, 1980; a colorful article by Daniel Goldberg entitled "Mesiras Nefesh" in the same Journal, Winter, 1978; the *Yud-Beis* Tammuz issues of this and other English-language *Chabad-Lubavitch* publications such as *Di Yiddishe Heim*; and the pioneering account in English, "The Arrest and Liberation of the Lubavitcher Rebbe," by Rabbi Nissan Mindel (Kehot, N.Y., 19??).

Major Hebrew sources include: *Sefer HaSichos 5680-5687 [1920-1927],* which appends contemporary documents; *Sefer HaToldos* of the Rebbe Rayatz (4 vols.; ed. Rabbi Chanoch Glitzenstein); and the *Yud-Beis* Tammuz issues of *Iton Kfar Chabad. Toldos Chabad BeRussia HaSovietis* (i.e., "The History of Chabad in the USSR, 1917-1950," compiled by Rabbi Shalom Dober Levin, chief librarian of the Central Library of Agudas Chassidei Chabad) is a comprehensive and illustrated treasure-house of information on the heroism and martyrdom of this period, based on private and official documents which in most cases are published here for the first time.

9. *Igros Kodesh* (Letters) of the Rebbe Rayatz, Vol. II, p. 420.
10. *Likkutei Sichos,* Vol. IV, p. 1322.

On other occasions[11] the Rebbe showed us how to perceive this date from a cosmic perspective. We have been promised by the prophet Zechariah[12] that in the Time to Come, the fast of the fourth month — i.e., the Seventeenth of Tammuz, commemorating the beginning of the Destruction — will be transformed into a day of gladness and joy. Ultimately, then, the innermost essence of this mournful fast will be revealed as a time of gladness and joy. Hence, the fact that Divine Providence positioned *Yud-Beis* Tammuz in the same month makes this festive date the beginning of the revelation of the Time to Come. May we soon be privileged to witness this with our own eyes!

Uri Kaploun

20 Menachem Av, 5756 [1996]
52nd *Yahrzeit* of Rabbi Levi Yitzchak Schneerson ז״ל

ACKNOWLEDGMENTS

The *maamarim* were translated by Rabbi Eliyahu Touger. The volume was edited by Uri Kaploun and guided through its editorial and publishing stages by Rabbi Yonah Avtzon, Director of Sichos In English. Yosef Yitzchok Turner invested his patience and professionalism in the layout and typography, and the cover was designed by Avrohom Weg. The cover photo was taken in Riga, Latvia, where the Rebbe Rayatz settled after leaving Russia in 1927.

NOTE

The source references which appeared in the body of the original Hebrew texts were left in place in the translation, and likewise, the original Hebrew footnotes appear at the foot of the English pages. Footnotes that were added in the English edition are enclosed by square brackets, as also are explanatory or connecting passages interpolated in the body of the translated text.

---

11. *Sefer HaSichos 5748 [1988]*, Vol. II, pp. 507, 531, and elsewhere.
12. Cf. *Zechariah* 8:19.

Maamar	מאמר
VeKibeil HaYehudim	וקבל היהודים
5687 [1927]	תרפ"ז

"The Jews accepted
what they had already begun…"

2   DEFIANCE AND DEVOTION

[One historic Purim Katan, hundreds of chassidim crowded into the modest wooden Lubavitcher *shul* that used to stand in the grounds of the imposing synagogue that still dominates Archipova Street in Moscow. Every single man clearly knew that the presence there of the Rebbe Rayatz and his own presence there endangered the lives of them all. (And in fact, exactly four months later, on 15 Sivan, the Rebbe himself together with many of those present was arrested.) For the year was 1927, and they all knew that planted amongst them were secret agents of the dreaded NKVD. To make things worse, the fearlessly "counter-revolutionary" discourse they were about to hear urged them to defy the Haman of their own days, and to prepare themselves to sacrifice their lives, quite literally, in order to keep the underground Torah classes open for the last hope of Israel – their own little children.

Some nine years later, in a letter written in Otvotzk, dated 1 Kislev 5697 [1936] and addressed to his Secretary for Educational Affairs, Rabbi H.M.A. Hodakov ע״ה, the Rebbe Rayatz himself described the events of that day:[1]

"...On Purim Katan, 5687 [1927], which fell on a Wednesday, I was in Moscow. The chassidim and the *temimim (May they live and be well!)* organized a *farbrengen* to be held in the Lubavitcher *shul.* That same morning I was informed that investigations were being made concerning me at my lodgings in the

---

1. *[Igros Kodesh* (Letters) of the Rebbe Rayatz, ed. R. Shalom Dober Levin (Kehot, N.Y.; Heb.), Vol. IV, pp. 16-17.*]*

Sibirski Hotel. A secret agent was already counting my steps. Early in the evening I received news from Leningrad that *(May we never know of such news!)* a person close to me[2] had been arrested. In fact, [among the chassidim,] fears were being expressed concerning me. Nevertheless, I did not want to cancel the *farbrengen.*

"The *farbrengen* was held at the appointed hour. I delivered the *maamar* which begins with the words, *VeKibeil HaYehudim Eis Asher Heicheilu.* The concept of self-sacrifice for the sake of the Torah and its *mitzvos* is mentioned there several times. I placed particular emphasis on those passages, ignoring the fact that the very walls had ears.... Later, in the course of the *farbrengen,* I repeated those words with an emphasis intended to arouse the hearts [of my listeners to action], in keeping with the needs of those days...."]

I

[The concluding passages of *Megillas Esther* record that after the miracle of Purim,] — וקבל היהודים אשר החלו לעשות — "The Jews accepted what they had already begun."[3] [This verse can be interpreted to mean that] at this time, in the era of exile, the Jews accepted [and internalized the process of spiritual progress that] they had begun previously, at the time of the Giving of the Torah. This interpretation echoes the teaching of our Sages (*Shabbos* 88a) on the verse,[4] קימו וקבלו היהודים — "The Jews affirmed and accepted..." The Sages understand this verse to mean that "they now

---

2. [R. Elchanan Dov ("Chonye") Marozov, secretary of the Rebbe Rayatz.]
3. [*Esther* 9:23.]
4. [*Ibid.*, v. 27.]

affirmed what they had already accepted [when the Torah was given]." [I.e., though the Jewish people had willingly accepted the Torah at Mount Sinai, it was not affirmed as an intrinsic, unalterable part of their beings until the events of Purim.]

On the surface, this is an inconceivable statement. At the time of the Giving of the Torah, the Jews had attained the loftiest heights of redemption, the most elevated levels of liberty and freedom. [Furthermore,] they had witnessed numerous signs and wonders during their exodus from Egypt; i.e., they had observed how the Divine power and life-energy which transcends the natural order became discernible and visible within nature itself. In particular, [this was revealed] at the splitting of the Red Sea.[5] When they reached Mount Sinai they had thus attained the ultimate peaks, and there they apprehended G-dliness through direct sense-perception.

Exile represents the absolute opposite. "We do not see our signs,"[6] for the G-dly light and life-energy are not at all apparent. On the contrary, "darkness covers the earth,"[7] [as the Divine light is obscured] in a manifold sequence of self-contractions, concealments and veilings.

All the exiles resemble the exile in Egypt,[8] of which it is written,[9] "They did not listen to Moshe because of their dwindled spirits and hard toil." [I.e.,] their back-breaking labors[10] [deadened their receptiveness to Moshe's message]. The same applies to every man in all other exiles. "With his

---

5. [As the Sages taught, a mere maidservant witnessed more at the Sea than did the prophets [in their visions]; cf. *Mechilta* and *Rashi* on *Shmos* 15:2.]
6. [*Tehillim* 74:9. The verse is referring to the signs and wonders of Divine revelation which are absent in the times of exile.]
7. [*Yeshayahu* 60:2.]
8. See *Bereishis Rabbah* 15:5, s.v. *Kol hamalchiyos*. This concept is explained at the beginning of *Parshas Shmos* in *Torah Or*.
9. [*Shmos* 6:9.]
10. [*Ibid.* 1:13-14.]

very soul he brings his bread,"¹¹ confronting many trials that challenge his observance of the Torah and its *mitzvos*. With the sweat of his brow, toiling arduously from the time he rises in the morning until the late hours of the night, he has time for neither prayer nor Torah study. He makes his way through his day with a troubled mind. "In the morning [he says], 'If only it were night,' and in the evening [he says], 'If only it were morning.'"¹² [Indeed, these pressures] leave people confused throughout the day and night.

In particular, in Haman's era, [in addition to the difficulties of earning a livelihood, the exile threatened our very existence. Haman] rose up against us to annihilate us, "to destroy, kill, and exterminate all the Jews, young and old,"¹³ without leaving a remnant or survivor, heaven forbid.

On that verse the *Midrash Rabbah* (7:13) comments: "[Haman] said, 'Surely I will begin by striking at these children.'" In order to carry out his wicked designs to destroy the Jewish people, heaven forbid, he would begin [by attacking] *tinokos shel beis rabban*, the children who study Torah.

There is an allusion to this in the verse,¹⁴ "And it came to pass in the days of Achashverosh...."

In *Midrash Rabbah*¹⁵ on this verse, our Sages comment:

> The phrase ויהי בימי ("And it came to pass in the days of...") always introduces a period of distress.
>
> For example, it is written,¹⁶ "And it came to pass in the days of Achaz...." What calamity transpired

---

11. [*Mussaf* of Rosh HaShanah (*Machzor*, p. 144) and Yom Kippur; cf. *Eichah* 5:9.]
12. [Cf. *Devarim* 28:67.]
13. [*Esther* 3:13.]
14. [*Ibid.* 1:1.]
15. [Prologue to *Esther Rabbah*, sec. 11.]
16. [*Yeshayahu* 7:1.]

then? [Achaz said,] "If there are no kids, there will be no goats.... If there are no children, there will be no adults; if there are no adults, there will be no scholars; if there are no scholars, there will be no sages; if there are no sages, there will be no elders; if there are no elders, there will be no Torah; if there is no Torah, there will be no synagogues and houses of study. And if there are no synagogues and houses of study, the Holy One, blessed be He, will not cause His presence to rest in the world."

What did he do? He locked all the synagogues and houses of study so that the Torah would not be studied.... Why was he called Achaz [which means "to hold fast"]? Because he firmly closed all the synagogues and houses of study.

[R. Yaakov bar Abba, speaking in the name of R. Acha, derived a lesson from the words of the prophet Yeshayahu:[17] "I have waited on G-d, Who hides His face from the House of Yaakov, and I have hoped for Him."

Referring to the edict of Achaz, he declared: "Never has Israel known such a dire hour; as it is written,[18] 'I will surely hide My face on that day, on account of all the evil....'] And since that hour *I have hoped for Him*, for it is written,[19] '[The Torah] will not be forgotten from the mouths of his descendants.'"

[And in this spirit too Yeshayahu challenged King Achaz:] "What success will you have?" (I.e.: What will you achieve by locking up synagogues and houses of study? Your intent is that, heaven forbid, the Torah will be forgotten by the Jewish people,

---

17. [Ibid. 8:17.]
18. [Devarim 31:18.]
19. [Ibid. 31:21.]

who will thus be separated from G-d. However, your endeavors will bear no fruit, because —) "Behold, I and the children whom G-d has given me as signs and wonders in Israel"[20] [will prevent that from happening].

Now were these his children?! Surely they were only his students! This, then, is the source which teaches us that a person's student is called his son.

Through these children, Yeshayahu rebuilt the ruin wrought by Achaz. This is what is meant by the words, "From that time 'I have hoped for Him,' for it is written, '[The Torah] will not be forgotten from the mouths of his descendants.'" For *tinokos shel beis rabban* are the foundation that enables "Your nation all [to be] righteous."[21]

Synopsis

The above chapter speaks of the lofty stature of [the Jews' spiritual attainments] and the exalted revelations [they experienced] during the Exodus from Egypt, the splitting of the Red Sea, and the Giving of the Torah. These are [contrasted with their] awesome descent and lowly spiritual level in the time of exile.

Haman's decree to (heaven forbid) destroy [the Jewish people] begins with *tinokos shel beis rabban*, for these children are the foundation of the Jewish people.

II

On this basis, we can understand the verse,[22] "Out of the mouths of babes and sucklings, You established the strength... to silence the enemy and the avenger." On the

---

20. *[Yeshayahu 8:18.]*
21. [Cf. *Ibid.* 60:21.]
22. *[Tehillim 8:3.]*

surface, the verse is problematic. Combating an enemy and, how much more so, one who seeks revenge, requires people of great strength and courage who are trained in the tactics of war.

[To explain:] An enemy is one who openly [displays his] hatred, while a person who seeks revenge is one who hides [his] hatred, but schemes [for revenge]. Furthermore, an enemy fights openly, and thus there are two camps, one pitted against the other. In contrast, revenge is taken only by one who is stronger than his adversary; i.e., for whatever reason, he is stronger, and seeks to take revenge against him.

Furthermore, in regard to war, there are certain accepted rules and conventions which limit the scope of one's activity. In contrast, a person who seeks revenge ignores these conventions entirely. To destroy an enemy and, how much more so, a person who is eager and — for some reason — able to take revenge, requires strong and courageous individuals who are able to withstand the throes of battle.

If so, why is it that "[the strength...] to silence the enemy and the avenger" derives from "babes and sucklings"? This is inconceivable. How can babes and sucklings with their minimal power nullify an enemy and even an avenger?

The concept can be explained as follows. It is written,[23] "'Not by might and not by power, but by My spirit,' says the L-rd of Hosts." ["My spirit"] refers to the revelation of the Divine Name *Havayah*[24] that takes place within every member of the Jewish people.

---

23. [*Zechariah* 4:6.]
24. [*Havayah* refers to the Name of G-d (י-ה-ו-ה), which may not be pronounced and is referred to by reading the letters in altered order.]

Thus it is specifically "from the mouths of babes and sucklings," from the breath of the *tinokos shel beis rabban*,[25] that "You established strength," for "There is no strength other than Torah."[26] And it is this strength that can negate an enemy and even an avenger.

[To return, however, to the question posed originally:] How is it possible that in the days of Haman, who desired (heaven forbid) to destroy [the Jewish people] when they were on a very low spiritual rung, that they were able to "affirm what they had already undertaken" when the Torah was given?

For, [as was pointed out above,] at Mount Sinai the Jews were on a high spiritual plane, as it is written,[27] "Face to face I spoke to you." *[Panim*, here translated as "face," also means "inner dimension." In that light, the verse can be interpreted, "My inner dimension was communicated to you and became your inner core."*]* Thus, as is known from other sources,[28] through this [process of communication,] the name *Havayah* was implanted within each and every Jew.

[The uniqueness of the Jews' level at the time the Torah was given is also expressed by our Sages' statement,[29] that "G-d] held the mountain over them like a tub," [so that they felt compelled to accept the Torah]. As interpreted elsewhere,[30] this statement means that there was [such a powerful] revelation [of G-dliness] from above [that the people had no choice but to accept the Torah].

---

25. [See *Shabbos* 119b.]
26. See *Vayikra Rabbah* 31:5 and *Yalkut Shimoni, Beshalach*, sec. 244; see also *Zevachim* 116a. Accordingly, the statement of *Kehilas Yaakov, Maareches Oz* ("We have not found a source in the teachings of the Sages [for the association of *oz* ('strength') with Torah]") is problematic.
27. [*Devarim* 5:4.]
28. See *Likkutei Torah*, at the beginning of *Parshas Re'eh*.
29. [*Shabbos* 88a.]
30. See *Torah Or, Megillas Esther, Chayav Inesh Livsumei*, ch. 4.

[These concepts reinforce the question mentioned above: Why is the Jews' declaration] *Naaseh venishma* ("We will [first] fulfill and we will [then] listen") considered only the *acceptance* [of the Torah and thus incomplete], while the affirmation [of the Jews' connection to the Torah] was actually realized only in the time of the exile, when they suffered extreme stress, heaven forbid? [How is it possible that it was specifically then that] "they affirmed what they had already accepted"?

Synopsis

An enemy engages in open combat, while a person who seeks revenge schemes in hiding. Both enemies and avengers are overcome by *tinokos shel beis rabban*. In this manner, we can understand the verse, "Out of the mouths of babes and sucklings, You established the strength... to silence the enemy and the avenger."

The question is raised: How is it possible that it was while under the threat of [Haman's] edict that the Jews confirmed in actual [life] what was, at the time of the giving of the Torah, accepted only in the sphere of potential? [How could the Jews have reached a higher rung of service in exile?]

III

This concept [can be explained as follows]: It is written,[21] "Your people are all righteous (*tzaddikim*).... They are the branch of My planting, the work of My hands, in which I take pride." By virtue of the source of their souls, the entire Jewish people are at the level of *tzaddikim*. This is the message of the verse, "Your people are all righteous." "Your people," G-d's people, who were conceived and born in holiness and purity as prescribed by the Torah, are at the level of *tzaddikim*.

On the surface, [this statement is problematic because] the level of the *tzaddik*[31] is elevated indeed.[32] How is it possible for each and every member of the Jewish people to reach this level in actual life to the extent that he is "a branch of My planting, the work of My hands, in which I take pride," [as expressed by] children and grandchildren who are involved in Torah study?

In particular, [one might ask: How could this level have been attained] in the time of exile, when Haman stood over the people with the intent to destroy and kill [them], heaven forbid? And despite this, they stood up with self-sacrifice and gathered together at that very time to study Torah in public.

Thus *Midrash Rabbah* [9:4] relates that Mordechai gathered together 22,000 students, and when the tyrant, the wicked Haman, approached them, they felt no fear whatsoever, declaring that whether [their fate be] life or death, they would remain bound to the Torah. They were willing to accept any punishment at all, to the point of actual self-sacrifice, as long as they would not be separated from the Torah.

On the surface, it is most remarkable that in such a bitter exile, heaven forbid, when the king had promoted and elevated the wicked Haman, the persecutor of the entire Jewish people, the Jews would be able to express such self-sacrifice.

[In resolution, we can explain]: On the verse,[33] "There was a Jewish man...," the *Midrash Rabbah* [6:2] relates that "in his generation, Mordechai [served a function] equivalent to [that served by] Moshe in his generation. Just as

---

31. [Cf. *Tanya*, chs. 1 and 10.]
32. See *Zohar* I, 93a; *Or HaTorah* by the *Tzemach Tzedek*, at the beginning of *Parshas Noach*.
33. [Esther 2:5.]

Moshe warded off potential disaster, so too did Mordechai.... Just as Moshe taught the Torah to the Jewish people, so too did Mordechai...."

Thus, it was through [Mordechai's influence] that the source of the souls of the Jewish people shone forth openly. And it was with this power that the Jews stood up with self-sacrifice in their practical observance of the Torah and its *mitzvos*.

[To explain Mordechai's influence in greater depth:] It is written,[34] ואתה תצוה את בני ישראל ויקחו אליך שמן זית זך כתית למאור להעלות נר תמיד — "And you [Moshe] shall command the Children of Israel to bring you pure oil, crushed for the light...to keep a constant light burning."

[This verse raises several questions:]

[1.] We must understand why the Torah uses different phraseology here than in regard to the other commandments.[35] Generally, when Moshe is given a command to convey to the Jews, he is told, "Command the Children of Israel." Why does the above verse state, "And *you* shall command the Children of Israel"?

[2.] Why were the Jews commanded to bring the olive oil to [Moshe]?[36] Since the lights were in fact lit by Aharon, it would seemingly be appropriate that the oil be brought to him. Why, then, does the Torah say that the oil should be brought "to you," [to Moshe]?

[3.] Also, the expression "crushed for the light" (כתית למאור) is problematic. The oil used for the lights simply had to be pure. Why [does the Torah mention that] it had to be crushed?

---

34. [*Shmos* 27:20.]
35. [See also *Sefer HaMaamarim 5689*, p. 163.]
36. [See also *Torah Or*, at the beginning of *Parshas Tetzaveh* (p. 81a).]

[4.] The expression "for the light" (למאור) also raises questions. Seemingly, it would have been more appropriate to say, "to illumine" (להאיר).

[5.] Also, we must understand what is meant by the expression, "a constant light" (נר תמיד). When [the Torah describes] the candles kindled by Aharon, it states[37] that [Aharon and his sons should prepare it so that it will burn] "from the evening until the morning." [Why then] does the Torah speak of "a constant light" in connection with Moshe?

[These questions can be resolved by explaining] their parallels in the service of G-d that takes place in the soul of man. For the ultimate intent [of creation] is that [every individual] become "a constant light," as it is written,[38] "The soul of man is a lamp of G-d." [The light of the soul] will then affect and illuminate all the worldly matters with which he is involved.

Synopsis

At the time of [Haman's] decree, the light in the soul of the Jewish people was revealed. With self-sacrifice, they stood firm in the face of challenges to their observance of the Torah and its *mitzvos*. [Their resolve was inspired] by Mordechai, who was equivalent to Moshe Rabbeinu, concerning whom it is written, "And you shall command the Children of Israel." This implies that he was granted the potential to connect the Jews to G-d, so that [each of them would shine as] "a constant light."

---

37. [*Shmos* 27:21.]
38. [*Mishlei* 20:27.]

IV

On this basis, [we can understand the use of the above expression], "And you shall command."[39] A commandment sets up a connection [between the one issuing the command and the one receiving it]. [This bond is reflected in the very words ציווי ("command") and צוותא ("together"), which share common root letters.]

"There is an extension of Moshe (אתפשטותא דמשה) in every generation."[40] [I.e., every generation has a *tzaddik* who performs a function similar to that performed by Moshe for his generation, and to him the Torah addresses itself, as follows:] "When 'you shall command the Children of Israel'" — i.e., when you [Moshe] connect [yourself with] the Children of Israel — "then 'they will bring you olive oil.'" I.e., the Jewish people, by serving G-d through studying Torah and observing the *mitzvos*, will thereby augment the light revealed at Moshe's level. And the result will be "a constant light."

To understand the above:[41] It is well known that Moshe is called "the faithful shepherd" (רעיא מהימנא),[42] because he nurtures the faith of the Jewish people. We, all of the Jewish people, believe in G-d with perfect faith to the point of actual self-sacrifice. Moshe is the shepherd who sustains and strengthens this faith.

A shepherd does not create anything new: he simply leads his flock to a place of fine pasture. "He gathers the

---

39. [See also *Torah Or, Tetzaveh* 82a; *Sefer HaMaamarim* 5679, p. 256; *Sefer HaMaamarim* 5689, pp. 175, 177.]
40. *Tikkunei Zohar, Tikkun* 69 (p. 114a); see also *Bereishis Rabbah* 56:7.
41. [The concepts outlined from this point until the conclusion of ch. 14 are based on *Sefer HaMaamarim* 5679, p. 247-274.]
42. [This idea is discussed in *Torah Or, Ki Sisa* 111a. Moshe Rabbeinu is referred to by the Hebrew original of this name (רועה נעמן) in the *Pesichta* to *Eichah Rabbah*, sec. 24; the above Aramaic version, also alluding to Moshe Rabbeinu, serves as the title of one of the component parts of the *Zohar*.]

lambs with his arm..., and gently leads those that are with sucklings."[43] He guides the little ones to the particular pasture that he has chosen as being best suited to their needs.

Thus *Midrash Rabbah* (*Shmos* 2:2) relates that Moshe would first take the tender lambs out to pasture among the softest shoots, then the older sheep to feed on the middling grass, and finally he would lead the sturdiest ones out to cope with the toughest grass.

"Said the Holy One, blessed be He: 'He who knows how to pasture sheep, each one according to his strength, should come to be a shepherd for My people.' This is implied by the verse,[44] 'From following the ewes with sucklings, He brought him to be the shepherd of Yaakov, His people.'"

Moshe is thus called a faithful shepherd, one who nourishes and strengthens our faith in G-d. As it is written,[45] "[Trust in G-d...] and *nurture*[46] faith," for faith must be nourished and sustained. Thus, the *Zohar* (III, 225b), [commenting on the above verse], speaks of "the sublime faith being sustained and fed through your [acts]." This means that faith needs to be strengthened, for "food is included in sustenance."[47] And this is the function of Moshe.

"There is an extension of Moshe in each generation." This refers to the leaders of the Jewish people, the "eyes of the congregation,"[48] the shepherds of Israel, who strengthen the people's faith in G-d [to the extent that] they are willing

---

43. [*Yeshayahu* 40:11.]
44. [*Tehillim* 78:71.]
45. [*Ibid.* 37:3.]
46. [The verb ורעה has been translated above in keeping with the thrust of the *maamar*. The commentaries offer different interpretations of its literal meaning.]
47. *Kesubbos* 57a. The relevance of this quotation here is not obvious.
48. [*Tanya — Iggeres HaKodesh*, Epistle 14 (p. 240), (cf. *Bamidbar* 15:24). See also *Shir HaShirim Rabbah* 1:15 (2).]

to actually sacrifice their lives for the observance of the Torah and its *mitzvos*.

To explain: The Jewish people are called "believers, the descendants of believers."[49] [They are called "believers,"] as it is written,[50] "And the people believed," and as it is likewise written,[51] "And they believed in G-d." They are called "the descendants of believers," for they are the descendants of Avraham, who is called [the personification of] faith, as it is written,[52] "And he believed in G-d." Moreover, there is a verse that says,[53] "[Come...] with me from Lebanon, look from the top of Amana." [Noting the resemblance between Amana, a mountain range in Lebanon, and *emunah*, the Hebrew for "faith," our Sages[54] interpret the above phrase:] "From Avraham, the first of the believers."

Our forefather Avraham was the first to open the path of faith [to the extent of] self-sacrifice, and this legacy of faith he bequeathed to his descendants.[55] This is the simple faith in G-d which is implanted in the heart of every Jew — that He permeates all worlds *(memaleh kol almin)* and transcends all worlds *(sovev kol almin)*, and that here is no place devoid of Him *(leis asar panui minei)*.[56]

Synopsis

Moshe as a "shepherd of faith." In each generation there is an extension of Moshe; these are the leaders of the Jewish people who strengthen their

---

49. *Shabbos* 97a. See also *Shmos Rabbah*, ch. 23; *Torah Or,* beginning of the *maamar* that opens, *Lehavin Inyan HaBerachos; Likkutei Torah LeShalosh Parshiyos.*
50. [*Shmos* 4:31.]
51. [Ibid. 14:31.]
52. [*Bereishis* 15:6; see *Shir HaShirim Rabbah* 4:8 (3).]
53. [*Shir HaShirim* 4:8.]
54. [*Shir HaShirim Rabbah*, loc. cit. (3)]
55. [See *Tanya*, ch. 18.]
56. [*Tikkunei Zohar, Tikkun* 57 (p. 91b); *Shaar HaYichud VehaEmunah*, ch. 7 (p. 166).]

faith in G-d, [making them aware that He] "permeates all worlds and transcends all worlds."

V

The Jewish people's faith reaches its peak at the level [of Divine light known as] *sovev kol almin*. [Appreciating G-d's manifestation at the level of *memaleh kol almin* does not challenge our resources of faith, for it can be understood intellectually.]

Avos DeRabbi Nasan[57] states: "[For] everything which the Holy One, blessed be He, created in the world [at large,] He created [a parallel] within man. He created forests in the world; as a parallel, he created hairs within man." [Similarly, that text] enumerates other phenomena created in the world which have parallels in man's [body]. For this reason our Sages[58] refer to man as a microcosm (*olam katan*), a world in miniature. It is likewise written,[59] "He placed the world in their hearts," for everything that exists in the world is purified and refined by man.

[Conversely,] the world is described[60] as a macrocosm (*guf gadol*), a large-scale body. For just as a man has 248 limbs, 365 sinews, hair, nails, and so on, parallels to these elements exist in the world at large. [The conception of the world as] a large-scale body also implies that it is animated by an indispensable source of life-energy. And, as we see, the world is alive. It is clear that trees and plants, for example, have a source of life-energy from which they derive their vitality.

---

57. [Ch. 31.]
58. *Midrash Tanchuma, Pekudei* 3; *Tikkunei Zohar*, beginning of *Tikkun* 69; see also *Likkutei Torah, Parshas Bamidbar*, the beginning of the *maamar* which opens, *Vehayah Mispar*.
59. [*Koheles* 3:11.]
60. *Moreh Nevuchim*, Vol. I, ch. 72.

This life-energy comes from the Divine light which is *memaleh kol almin,* focusing its [immanent] light and life-energy on each individual created being in a particularized manner. [This is implied by our Sages' statement,[61]] "Just as the soul permeates [lit., 'fills'] the body, so the Holy One, blessed be He, permeates [lit., 'fills'] the world." The manner in which the body (which is a world in miniature) derives its vitality from the soul, reflects the manner in which the world (which is a large-scale body) derives *its* life-energy. This life-energy [is beamed] in a particular manner, each individual being [receiving its own life-energy]. This parallels the manner in which the light and life-energy of the soul is enclothed in each limb individually.

[To elaborate on this analogy:] The light and life-energy of the soul which is enclothed in the body is manifest in three ways: it animates the head in a different manner from the way in which it animates the torso and the legs.

It goes without saying that the legs have a function to serve, for a perfect body comprises all the limbs, and this of course includes the legs. [Furthermore,] they are in a sense superior[62] to the rest of the body, for they support the head and raise it high. While it is the head that makes one person appear taller than another, it is the legs that in fact make the difference between them. Or, [to give another example,] while the difference between a person when seated and when standing erect is noticed in the height of his head, here too it is the legs that make the difference. Moreover, the feet conduct the head to places which it could never reach, if left to its own resources.

---

61. See *Berachos* 10a; *Vayikra Rabbah* 4:8; *Midrash Tehillim* on ch. 103. See also *Likkutei Torah,* beginning of *Parshas Emor.*
62. See the beginning of *Torah Or; Likkutei Torah,* beginning of *Parshas Nitzavim;* and elsewhere.

[The potential possessed by the legs can be understood within the context of the statement,[63] "The beginning is implanted in the end." This implies that] the ultimate source is more directly implanted in the legs than in the head [where it is openly] expressed.

This [concept is reflected in the following interpretation of the words spoken by Moshe Rabbeinu:[64]] שש מאות אלף רגלי העם אשר אנכי בקרבו — "Here I am in the midst of 600,000 people on foot." Moshe's spiritual level was that of the *Sefirah* called *Chochmah* ("wisdom"). The word "I" (*Anochi* in Hebrew) refers to the transcendent level of *Keser* (the highest of all *Sefiros*). The presence of *"Anochi"* within the "midst" of Moshe alludes to the revelation of *Keser* within *Chochmah*. This is made possible only because of the "600,000 people on foot" (literally, "the feet of the people").[65] It is thus the "feet of the people" which add light to Moshe. This is implied by the statement in the liturgy,[66] "Moshe rejoiced in the gift of his portion." [Why was he granted this portion? Our Sages explain that G-d said to Moshe,[67]] "I endowed you with greatness only for the sake of the Jewish people."

Synopsis

The world (which is a large-scale body) is refined through man (who is a world in miniature), for man understands and senses the Divine life-energy within the world because of the life-energy that animates his soul. [The Divine life-energy which one perceives is] the immanent, permeating light which is called *memaleh kol almin*.

---

63. [*Sefer Yetzirah* 1:7.]
64. [*Numbers* 11:21.]
65. [This concept is explained in the beginning of *Torah Or*, p. 1b.]
66. [The *Shabbos* morning prayers; *Siddur Tehillat HaShem,* p. 179.]
67. [*Berachos* 32a.]

Though the legs are the lowest components of the body, they are superior to the head inasmuch as they support it and raise it up. [The message of this analogy is explained within the context of an interpretation of the verse,] "Here I am in the midst of 600,000 people on foot."

VI

[An awareness of the spiritual power possessed by the "legs of the people," i.e., the common people, should inspire efforts to reach out to these people and motivate them to express this power.]

Our Sages taught,[68] גדול המעשה יותר מן העושה — "A person who causes another to perform [a *mitzvah*] is greater than the person who actually performs [the *mitzvah*]." The supporters of Torah study (תמכין דאורייתא) are thus more praiseworthy than the very scholars whom their contributions maintain.[69]

Furthermore, catalysts of this kind are to be esteemed not only in relation to financial support, but likewise in relation to spiritual charity. It is a commendable attainment indeed when, for example, a person establishes a regular session of communal Torah study, and the *Halachah* or *Aggadah* in question matches the level of the participants. Indeed, this attainment illustrates our Sages' interpretation of the verse,[70] "Hearken and listen Israel." [Noting the relationship between the words הסכת ("hearken") and כתה ("class"), they comment:[71]] "Set up classes and study the

---

68. [*Bava Basra* 9a.]
69. [See the *Rama, Yoreh Deah*, end of sec. 246:1, the Alter Rebbe's *Shulchan Aruch, Hilchos Talmud Torah* 3:4; *Zohar* III, top of p. 241b; *Sefer Ha-Maamarim 5696*, p. 72.]
70. [*Devarim* 27:9.]
71. [*Berachos* 63b.]

Torah together, for only in a group can the Torah be mastered."

Even those individuals who are capable of [independent,] advanced study should participate in these [communal] study sessions.[72] It goes without saying that the person who delivers such a class is both rewarded and spiritually elevated thereby. Beyond that, moreover, even the other participants are considered to have given spiritual charity. Since each man's presence strengthens his neighbor, each man there is a "supporter of Torah." And such efforts are all the more praiseworthy when [directed] to simple people.

Another [expression of the unique spiritual potential possessed by common people] is the power of *mesirus nefesh* ("self-sacrifice"), which is more [openly revealed] among simple people than among intellectuals and others with a developed understanding.[73]

From the above, it is obvious that the feet possess great qualities. Nonetheless, in regard to the light and life-energy which is enclothed in the body in [a revealed and] immanent manner, the middle portion of the body, the torso, is on a higher level than are the feet. [This is reflected by] the presence there of the heart and other internal organs on which a person's life depends. Even the slightest perforation[74] in them [could cause a person's death]. In contrast,

---

72. See the conclusion of Epistle 23 of *Iggeres HaKodesh*.
73. See the *maamarim* beginning *Ein HaKadosh-Baruch-Hu Ba* and *Ani Yesheinah*, in *Sefer HaMaamarim — Yiddish*.
74. [In its original halachic context, this phrase would mean that "even the tiniest perforation [renders them unfit]." The phrase is borrowed from the laws of *treifos*, which judge an animal unfit to be eaten if it has a physical blemish that will cause it to die within twelve months. If even the slightest perforation is found in one of eleven named organs (including the brain, the heart, the lungs, and the major organs of the digestive system), the animal is considered to be *treifah*. See *Mishneh Torah, Hilchos Shechitah* 6:1.]

the feet possess only one faculty, motor power, which is the lowest potential possessed by our souls.

[The faculties housed in the torso] are immeasurably more refined [than those of the feet. Firstly, our] emotions [are associated with the heart]. Even in regard to motor power, the hands [which are associated with the torso] manifest this potential in a far more developed manner than [is reflected in] the ability of the feet to walk. The feet can at best propel stones, a potential possessed by animals as well. In contrast, the power of movement in the hands is also expressed in the ability to write, which is a uniquely human potential, and likewise in the ability to draw.

Although these two last-mentioned skills are also expressions of the power of movement, which is the lowest of the potentials possessed by our souls, they represent the inner dimension of that potential; i.e., each of our potentials has an external dimension and an internal dimension.[75] For example, the external dimension of the potential of movement is expressed in walking and propelling [objects], while the internal dimension is expressed in writing and art.

To elaborate: Even when [the power of propulsion is interrelated with the power of thought, as in] the precise propulsion of an object, causing it to "hit its target to within a hair's-breadth without missing,"[76] and which requires thought and practice, the most prominent element is the actual deed. This is evidenced by the fact that after the power invested in the article that was thrown ceases, the

---

75. [The above concepts of "externality" (*chitzoniyus*) and "internality" (*pnimiyus*) can be explained as follows: The adjective "internal" describes a faculty that voices and communicates a person's personality and character. Thus the word *pnimiyus* relates to the word *panim* ("face"), which is that part of us in which these dimensions are expressed. In contrast, "external" describes those activities and aspects of our being that do not reflect these elements.]

76. [Cf. *Shoftim* 20:16.]

object naturally falls. In contrast, [the power of movement used in producing] a work of art is a garment, [i.e., a means of presentation,] for the intellect. Furthermore, we see how the intellect dominates [and controls] the [physical] power. For this reason, the fundamental beauty of a work of art is its content and its message and not the mere form presented. Thus, it reflects the inner dimension of the power of action.

Synopsis

"A person who causes another to perform [a *mitzvah*] is greater than the person who actually performs [the *mitzvah*]." This teaching of our Sages can be applied to the "supporters of Torah," those who with their money and their efforts encourage communal Torah study. Studying with the common people can be considered as spiritual charity.

The foot [and so too the common people it metaphorically represents] possesses great qualities. It is, however, the lowest of the [three divisions of the body, expressing our least developed] powers. [Even the power of movement which it does express, is surpassed by the power of movement in the hands, which are capable of producing] artistic creations that are garments for the intellect.

VII

Our emotional potentials are on a higher plane than even the inner dimension of the power of movement. This also holds true for [the limbs which are] the vessels [for these powers], as evidenced by the heart, which is the seat of the emotions.

Nevertheless, when compared to the head, even the torso is of lesser standing, for the head contains our most sophisticated capabilities — sight, hearing, taste and smell, and of course, the power of intellect in the brain. [Attaching this importance to the brain is not intended to minimize the importance of the heart. Indeed,] in regard to a person's life, the heart and the brain are equally vital. Just as it is impossible to live without a head, it is impossible to live without a heart.[77]

These aspects of man's external physical existence are also reflected in his inner life-potential, man's inner self. Thus our Sages (*Shabbos* 11a) state, "Any pain, but not a pained heart; any infirmity, but not an infirmity of the head."

A healthy person has both a brain and the heart [and modulates the influence of one with the other, as indicated by] the adage,[78] "There is no wise man like a man of experience." This refers to a person whose wisdom has stood by

---

77. The *Zohar* (III, 221b) states that without these organs, one cannot live "for even a moment." This position is also corroborated by the commentary of *Kesef Mishneh* on *Mishneh Torah, Hilchos Shechitah* 10:9, which states [that in his list of blemishes that would cause an animal to die within twelve months, *Rambam* did not mention the lack of a vital organ,] e.g., the heart or the brain, [because this is self-evident]. See also Responsa 74-77 of *Chacham Zvi*, which support this position].

There are, however, authorities who differ from *Chacham Zvi*. See the Responsa of *Maharamaz*, Responsum 33; *Kreisi U'Pleisi*, 40:4; *Panim Meiros*, Vol. I, sec. 23; *She'elas Yaavetz*, Vol. I, Responsum 121; HaRav Chayim *Or Zarua*, Responsum 146; *Mishbetzos Zahav*, at the conclusion of ch. 40; as well as other later authorities as quoted by *Darchei Teshuvah*, [*Yoreh Deah*, sec. 40].

There is some difficulty [with the statements in the *maamar*], for the *Tzemach Tzedek* favors the opinion of *Kreisi U'Pleisi*, who differs from *Chacham Zvi*. One may, however, resolve the difficulty by postulating that a human being [the subject of the statements in our *maamar*] differs in this respect from an animal [the subject of the halachic discussion above]. Alternatively, one can use the resolution offered by *Afudi* in his commentary to *Moreh Nevuchim*, Vol. I, ch. 73. See also [the commentary of the] *Yad Shaul, Yoreh De'ah*, loc. cit. At any rate, this is not the place for further discussion of the matter.

78. [See *Akeidah, Parshas Noach, Shaar* 14, Third Introduction.]

him [in his everyday experience], enabling him to carry out positive activity.

[To illustrate by contrast,] there are some people who have admirable powers of comprehension. They can understand what is true and good, but their wisdom is only an academic abstraction. It has no effect on the realm of action at all: the brain does not affect the heart and the heart is not influenced by the brain. [Such a person] understands what should be done, but [expressing these values] in actual life is another matter entirely.

True health involves both an active brain and an active heart, each one in its own sphere. The brain should thoroughly comprehend a concept with due breadth of scope. The heart should then translate this potential into actuality, refining the individual's emotions as dictated by his comprehension of [the intellectual blueprint].

Thus, the brain and the heart play equal roles in human life. Nevertheless, the brain surpasses the heart [because it is the brain which conveys the ideas that are actualized through the heart]. [A question concerning the dominance of the brain can be raised for] רעותא דליבא (lit., "the will of the heart," a person's innermost spiritual desire), which transcends his intellect, is expressed in the heart. This, however, reflects a level of the light and life-energy which transcends the life and light-energy that is enclothed within the body.

[To explain:] There are two levels of "the will of the heart":[79]

(a) That which is brought about by meditation (*hisbonenus*); i.e., though it is an innate and essential desire (*ratzon atzmi*), it is evoked by meditation. This refers to [an elevated level of meditation,] meditation on the *Or Ein Sof,*

---

79. See the series of discourses (*hemshech*) of Rosh HaShanah, 5710, ch. 23 (*Kuntreis* 71).

the Infinite Light which transcends *hishtalshelus,* the entire scheme of spiritual existence. This meditation is a function of the brain and it finds expression in an arousal of the heart.

(b) The elemental will of the soul insofar as it exists in the core of the soul, which is intrinsically bound with the [infinite] essence of the *Ein Sof,* blessed be He. This is the bond alluded to by the phrase in the liturgy,[80] "clinging and cleaving to You."

[Both these levels] reflect the light and life-energy of the soul insofar as they transcend the light and life-energy enclothed in the body. [I.e., although this essential will is occasionally revealed within our lives, we have no control over it. It is an expression of the essence of our souls which entirely supersedes our normal conscious processes.] In regard to the light and life-energy of the soul which is enclothed in the body, [i.e., with regard to our ordinary conscious processes,] the head is the most elevated component of the body.

Synopsis

A person's life depends on both the brain and the heart. [The usual order of our conscious processes is that] intellectual comprehension leads to the refinement of the emotions in the heart.

There are two levels of "the will of the heart." The superiority of the heart [in the service of G-d] is expressed in "the will of the heart"; the superiority of the mind [in the service of G-d] is expressed in the realm of comprehension.

---

80. [The *piyyut* recited for *Hoshanos* on the third day of Sukkos.]

VIII

Just as the soul which permeates (lit., "fills") the body is manifest in three general ways, [depending on whether it is animating] the head, the torso, or the feet, similarly [the light and life-energy of] the spiritual worlds [is manifest] at three levels, [depending on whether it is animating] the World of *Beriah,* the World of *Yetzirah,* or the World of *Asiyah.*

[Now it is true that there are more than three spiritual worlds.] Thus, on the verse,[81] ועלמות אין מספר — "And maidens without number," we are taught, "Do not read עלמות ('maidens') but עולמות ('worlds');[82] i.e., there is an utterly unlimited number of spiritual worlds. Nevertheless, these [may be classified in] three general categories, the Worlds of *Beriah, Yetzirah* and *Asiyah.* This division is reflected in the statement,[83] "The Supernal Mother [i.e., the *Sefirah* of *Binah*] makes her home in [the Divine] Throne [i.e., the World of *Beriah*]; the six *Sefiros* [are to be found] in [the World of] *Yetzirah,* and [the *Sefirah* of] *Malchus* [is to be found] in [the World of] *Asiyah.* However, the various worlds may still be described as being innumerable and unbounded because the [Divine] light and life-energy [which animates them] divides into a multitude of levels according to the nature of each world.

This [division] characterizes the light of *memaleh kol almin,* the Divine light which enclothes itself in the worlds. It is a ray of [Divine] light that undergoes a manifold process of self-contraction and [self-]concealment.

[This process is alluded to in the verse,[84]] מלכותך מלכות כל עולמים — "Your Kingship is a kingship over all worlds";

---

81. [*Shir HaShirim* 6:8.]
82. *Zohar* III, 71b; Introduction to *Tikkunei Zohar,* 14b.
83. *Tikkunei Zohar* 6.
84. [*Tehillim* 145:13.]

i.e., all the worlds come into being through the attribute of *Malchus* ("kingship"). [The *Sefirah* of] *Malchus* of [the World of] *Atzilus* is the light and the life-energy for the three Worlds of *Beriah, Yetzirah* and *Asiyah*. Nevertheless, this light — the light of *Malchus* of *Atzilus* that vitalizes the Worlds of *Beriah, Yetzirah,* and *Asiyah* — is merely a ray. Only the external dimension of *Malchus* is transmitted, and this transmission is [indirect; i.e., its influence is] interrupted by the *parsah* [lit., "curtain"][85] that separates the World of *Atzilus* from the Worlds of *Beriah, Yetzirah* and *Asiyah*.

This [transmission of influence emanating from *Malchus*] is of two levels: there is an influence from "nearby" and an influence from "afar". A king, by way of analogy, conducts his country by means of two opposite potentials. [On the one hand,] the very essence and foundation of sovereignty is the attribute of exalted majesty. For this reason [a king] must be exalted and uplifted, for leadership involves majesty, [i.e., raising oneself above one's subjects, transcending their particular situations].

[On the other hand, the second dimension of kingship is reflected in the verse,[86]] מלך במשפט יעמיד ארץ — "A king establishes the land with judgment." The fundamental concern of a ruler is his country's welfare, and this concern is expressed through [careful] judgment concerning all its affairs. Thus, [the people accepted Shlomo as a king and] "stood in awe [of him], because they saw that the wisdom of G-d was within him, [enabling him] to execute judgment."[87]

---

85. [The *parsah* is a figure of speech signifying the Divine power of self-concealment that allows for a transition from the World of *Atzilus*, which is identified with G-d Himself, to the World of *Beriah*, where the potential for seemingly independent existence is first manifest.]
86. [*Mishlei* 29:4.]
87. [*I Melachim* 3:28.]

[In contrast to the majestic stance previously described,] which implies distance, judgment [entails a closeness between a king and his subjects, for it] involves investigating and examining the entire range of particular elements that comprise [the task of] administering [a country]. And it is through [the fusion of] these two approaches that [the administration of] a country is maintained.

Similarly, in the analog [in the spiritual realms, these two approaches] represent the two levels of *Malchus*: (a) Influence transmitted through [metaphorical] distance; [i.e., the dimension of majesty as reflected in the verse,[88]] "And the sea [was set] upon them from above"; (b) Influence transmitted through [metaphorical] closeness. As explained elsewhere,[89] this refers to the ray of Divine light that is transmitted despite the *parsah* separating the World of *Atzilus* from the Worlds of *Beriah, Yetzirah,* and *Asiyah*.

Synopsis

Beriah, Yetzirah and *Asiyah* are three [general categories of] worlds, whereas the expression, "worlds without number," refers to the innumerable levels that exist within each of these worlds. This [multiplicity is a function of] the [immanent and particularized] light of *memaleh kol almin*.

"Your kingship is a kingship over all the worlds." [This phrase signifies that all the worlds receive their Divine influence from the attribute of *Malchus*, kingship.] This influence [of life-giving energy] is transmitted through two approaches, one involving distance and one involving closeness. These ap-

---

88. *[Ibid. 7:25.* Though in this particular context "the sea" denotes a reservoir of water in the *Beis HaMikdash,* "the sea" in its usual sense alludes in the language of *Chassidus* to the hidden, transcendent dimension of *Malchus*. It is described as being set "upon them from above," i.e., projecting the Divine attribute of majesty upon the world.*]*
89. See *Likkutei Torah, Shir HaShirim* 8b ff., and other sources.

proaches are illustrated by the analogy of [a king who] rules [his country by employing] both majesty [i.e., influence transmitted through distance] and judgment [i.e., influence transmitted through closeness].

IX

In contrast [to the light of *memaleh kol almin* discussed above], the light of *sovev kol almin* is not enclothed in the worlds in an immanent manner. Rather, it grants life to the worlds as it transcends them.

The verse,[90] את השמים ואת הארץ אני מלא — "I fill the heavens and the earth," [though speaking of G-d's own Being, does not contradict the concept of His transcendence]. As explained in ch. 38 of *Tanya*, the phrase *sovev [kol almin]* does not signify a Divine light that encompasses the worlds from above. Rather, this dimension of G-dliness is present within every element of existence and within the innermost depths of this material world, though it is not "enclothed and secured" within the world.

[Being "enclothed and secured" would mean that it would be revealed by the medium which enclothes it; that medium would dominate it and define the nature of its revelation. For example,] the life-energy of *memaleh kol almin* is enclothed and secured within the worlds. [Therefore, the G-dly nature of this life-energy is not openly revealed and what is apparent is physical life. In contrast, the light] of *sovev kol almin* [exists within the worlds, though] without being "enclothed and secured" in them; as it is written,[91] כי נשגב שמו לבדו — "His Name is exalted alone." I.e., [even] His Name is exalted and majestic, transcending [the worlds].

---

90. *[Yirmeyahu 23:24.]*
91. *[Tehillim 148:13.]*

The above reflects our faith, the faith of the entire Jewish people, that the *Or Ein Sof*, the Infinite Light, grants life to the worlds at two levels, *sovev kol almin* and *memaleh kol almin*.

[More specifically,] the essence of faith [relates to the level of] *sovev kol almin*. [In regard to the level of] *memaleh kol almin*, [faith is not required, because] it is possible to *comprehend* [the existence of this manifestation of G-dliness as powerfully] as if it were actually seen; as it is written,[92] מבשרי אחזה אלו-ה — "From my flesh, I behold G-d." From his own being, every man can appreciate the manner [in which G-dliness is manifest] in the world. Everyone comprehends that there is a life-force that endows him with life, for [his] body is alive — not in the sense that the body merely houses a living entity by virtue of which it is alive, but rather in the sense that the body itself is alive. From this, the individual knows that this life of the body stems from the life-force which animates it, [for when the body is cut off from that life-force, it exists without life].

One knows well that this life-force is manifest G-dliness for it can be clearly seen that an entity which is not manifest G-dliness does not live. For example, the body is an entity in its own right, a *yesh*. It does not live without the soul, (and merely exists by virtue of an edict of the Supernal Understanding, which alone maintains it in existence). In contrast, the soul lives because it is G-dliness, for life is G-dliness; as it is written,[93] וה' אלקים אמת הוא אלקים חיים — "And G-d, the L-rd, is true; He is the living G-d."

[Since life emanates from G-dliness,] the medium for life is *bittul*, self-nullification. [This is evident from the

---

92. *[Iyov* 19:26. Regarding the above translation, see *Likkutei Torah, Emor* 31b, and *Vaes'chanan* 4a; *Likkutei Dibburim*, Vol. II, p. 332b ff. (and in English translation: Vol. III, ch. 19, sec. 9).]
93. [*Yirmeyahu* 10:10.]

verse,[94] יראת ה' לחיים — "The fear of G-d [leads] to life." Thus, the angels live and exist forever because of their great awe and *bittul,* as explained elsewhere.[95] Thus, since life is manifest G-dliness, the medium for attaining life is *bittul.*

[Based on the above, one can conclude that] faith is not necessarily the most appropriate means of apprehending [the immanent light of] *memaleh kol almin.* Rather, the essence of faith relates to [the transcendent light of] *sovev kol almin,* which is not [openly] comprehended or felt.

Synopsis

The light of *sovev kol almin* is a transcendent [light] which is not enclothed within the world. The Jewish people's faith [relates to the level of] *memaleh kol almin,* but in essence [relates more to the light of] *sovev kol almin.*

The light of *memaleh kol almin* can be perceived; as it is written, "From my flesh, I perceive [G-d]." The medium by which the Divine life-force may be received is *bittul.* The [eternal] existence of the angels is a result of their *bittul.*

X

[These two levels] are reflected in the declarations [of faith] that we make daily. The first is, [שמע ישראל...] ה' אחד — ["Hear, O Israel,...] G-d is one."[96] The second is, ברוך שם כבוד מלכותו לעולם ועד — "Blessed be the Name of His glori-

---

94. [*Mishlei* 19:23; cf. the commentary of *Metzudas David.*]
95. [See the series of *maamarim* beginning *BeShaah SheHikdimu, 5672,* Vol. II, p. 684.]
96. [*Devarim* 6:4.]

ous kingdom forever and ever."[97] [These declarations represent] an acceptance [of G-d's sovereignty] and [an expression of our] faith in [G-d's manifestation as] *memaleh kol almin* and *sovev kol almin*.

Our faith in [these two expressions of G-dliness] corresponds to the two levels of *bittul* alluded to in the verse,[98] א-ל דעות ה׳ — "The L-rd is a G-d of knowledge." [The plural form of דעות, the word here translated "knowledge," leads to the interpretation[99] that] there are two planes in the knowledge [of G-d].

From the perspective of the lower plane of knowledge (*daas tachton*), our lowly realm [is perceived as being] *yesh* ("something"), while the higher realms [are perceived as being] *ayin* ("nothing"). That is to say: Since the existence of created beings [in this world] is seen, revealed and felt, they are called *yesh*, while the G-dliness that brings [them] into being is called *ayin* because it is not grasped.

[This term is used because] a created being calls whatever he cannot grasp — *ayin*, i.e., not what he himself is. He himself is a tangible entity, whereas the [Divine] life-energy is not an entity of that nature. He therefore calls it *ayin*, i.e., not what he is.

[We cannot say that by the word *ayin* he simply means to say "nothing", implying that the Divine life-force does not exist, because man] does perceive and recognize that there is a life-force [which maintains his existence] and, indeed, is the essence [of existence]. Nevertheless, since [that life-force] does not exist in the same manner as he does, he calls it *ayin*, [something he cannot perceive].

[In contrast, from the perspective of] the higher plane of knowledge (*daas elyon*), the spiritual realms are [perceived

---

97. [*Pesachim* 56a.]
98. [*I Shmuel* 2:3.]
99. [See *Tikkunei Zohar*, *Tikkun* 69.]

as being] *yesh,* true existence, while the lower level [i.e., material existence] is [perceived as being] *ayin,* a nonentity. From this perspective, the *Ein Sof* is the true existence and the levels below are *ayin,* for "before Him, everything is of no consequence."[100]

It is a familiar concept[101] that these two approaches exist within G-dliness itself. [The lower plane of knowledge is not merely the perspective of man: it has its source in the graduated sequence of the revelation of Divine light.] The ray of G-dliness which is the source for [the existence of] the worlds operates according to the lower level of knowledge. Since it is the source for the worlds, it (so to speak) considers the worlds' existence significant [and thus, the world can be considered *yesh*].

[To explain: The level of G-dliness which serves as the source for the world is the *Sefirah* of *Malchus,* kingship. However,] "A king cannot exist without a people";[102] i.e., the attribute of kingship presupposes the existence of a nation which submits itself to a king. [In the analog, the submission of the people parallels] the worlds' *bittul* [to the G-dly life-force which brings them into being]. [The analogy of a kingdom is appropriate because it also reveals the nature of this *bittul,*] which is *bittul hayesh,* [a *bittul* in which the self-effacing entity still retains its identity. As with subjects who submit themselves to a king, deference is paid to a higher authority; this does not, however, nullify their own individual existence.]

---

100. *[Zohar* I, 11b; cf. *Daniel* 4:32.]
101. See *Likkutei Torah, Shemini Atzeres* 83a, and *Shir HaShirim* 47b, and other sources.
102. [Rabbeinu Bachye, on *Bereishis* 38:30; *Shaar HaYichud VehaEmunah,* ch. 7.]

We are not referring to *bittul bimetzius*, utter self-nullification to the extent that one's personal identity is effaced entirely, for on such a level, there can be no concept of kingship, [which by definition involves rule over separate entities]. Thus, the approach is one of *bittul hayesh*. This is reflected in the [relationship between] the created beings which are *yesh*, independently existing entities, and the *ayin*, the Divine [life-force]. The faith and the understanding [of the created beings] cause them to be *batel* to the *ayin*, the Divine [life-force]. This *bittul*, however, is merely *bittul hayesh*.

[In contrast,] the higher plane of knowledge relates to *Or Ein Sof*, the Infinite Light, as it transcends the worlds, manifesting itself on the level of *sovev kol almin*. On this level [is manifest the higher plane of] knowledge which views the worlds as effacing themselves to the point of *bittul bimetzius*. [This is reflected in the expression,] "Before Him, everything is of no consequence."

It is, however, only "before Him," [i.e., only at the higher levels of G-dliness,] that "everything is of no consequence."[103] In contrast, in regard to the attribute of *Malchus*, [the lower Divine attribute which is the source for worldly existence,] "A king cannot exist without a people." [The people, in the analog,] the worlds, are significant, but they submit themselves [to Him].

It is faith that [produces] *bittul*. Thus, faith in the two levels of *memaleh kol almin* and *sovev kol almin* is [the source for] the two levels of *bittul* mentioned above. Our acceptance of these two levels of *bittul* is expressed in our statements, "G-d is one," and "Blessed be the Name of His glorious kingdom forever and ever." [In the *Shema*, the name used for G-d is *Havayah*, indicating that] the faith of

---

103. [See *Likkutei Torah, Acharei* 26a.]

the souls of the Jewish people is [directed to] the Name *Havayah*, [the transcendent dimension of G-dliness].

Faith, however, transcends [our ordinary conscious processes and is often not integrated within them]. [To illustrate this concept:] Our Sages taught,[104] "A thief calls on G-d before breaking in [to a house]." He believes in G-d; he believes that He nourishes and sustains all of His creatures, "providing bread for all flesh,"[105] and overseeing [the fortunes of] each and every creature individually. And it is because of this faith that He asks G-d, blessed be He, to help him and grant him success,[106] so that he too will have "bread to eat and clothing to wear."[107] In what, however, does he ask for success? — In stealing, and in not being caught in the act! Now this is a paradox indeed, asking G-d for help while flagrantly defying His will.

This inconsistency is possible because faith is far removed [from our ordinary conscious processes] and is not internalized within them. If the faith radiating in a man were to be integrated within him, he would find it impossible to defy G-d's will, to transgress the directives that come from His mouth. This paradoxical situation can exist only because faith stands beyond [our ordinary conscious processes].

Synopsis

Our faith [in G-d] as *memaleh kol almin* and *sovev kol almin* [brings about] two types of *bittul:* (a) the *bittul* associated with the lower plane of knowledge, *bittul hayesh,* [i.e., the created beings negate

---

104. *Berachos* 63a, as cited in *Ein Yaakov*. A note in *Pachad Yitzchak* (s.v. גנבא) records that this is the reading in the Portuguese edition of the *Talmud*.
105. [Cf. *Tehillim* 136:25.]
106. [Note by the publisher (of the Hebrew edition): The words "so that...for success?" are not in the original handwritten manuscript of the *maamar*.]
107. [*Bereishis* 28:20]

themselves] to the *ayin,* the ray of G-dliness which brings the worlds into existence; (b) the *bittul* associated with the higher plane of knowledge, *bittul bimetzius.*

Our acceptance of these two levels of *bittul* is expressed in our statements, "G-d is one," and "Blessed be the Name of His glorious kingdom forever and ever."

Faith, [however, by its very definition] transcends [our ordinary conscious processes]. [Therefore, it can lead to the paradox whereby] "a thief calls on G-d before breaking in."

XI

Every single person can find parallels [to such a paradox] — whether [as] grossly or perhaps more subtly — within his own personal situation. We ask for help from G-d, blessed be He, and yet the things we ask for may be utterly superfluous, serving merely to fulfill our desires. This is surely not His will, and thus such a person's situation parallels that of the thief [who prays] before breaking in [as mentioned above].

What causes such a situation? — A fundamental error which many people make regarding themselves. They are so convinced of their importance and personal worth that they think they deserve wealth [and other blessings]. Thus, [they rationalize,] they will be able to serve G-d through Torah study and prayer amidst prosperity.

[This, however, is only a rationalization.] In truth, their ultimate motivation is the wish that these material benefits fulfill their own desires — a motivation that does not reflect G-d's will at all.

[There are other more] subtle [expressions of the above paradox]. Commercial activity, for example, is intended to be a medium through which one can earn a livelihood. This medium must be pure; i.e., it should not involve the slightest trace of the prohibitions of falsehood, dishonesty, and the like. In fact, one's business dealings should be carried out in good faith[108] to the extent that one "speaks the truth in one's heart,"[109] as our Sages teach.[110]

Moreover, the overriding consideration should be that one's business dealings be carried out for the sake of heaven; i.e., one should be motivated by a Divine intent. It is true that permission has been granted to engage in business and to work, as it is written,[111] "Six days shall you work," and it is written,[112] "And G-d will bless you in all that you do," [implying that His blessing requires a certain measure of human activity which it will prosper and enhance].

Nevertheless, that activity itself is not the Divine intent underlying Creation.[113] Not for this was man created. On the contrary, the purpose for man's creation is [implied by the verse,[114]] "I made the world and I created man upon it." The word meaning "I created" (בראתי) is numerically equivalent to תרי"ג,[115] an acronym that alludes to the 613 *mitzvos*, for these are the reason for the world's creation.

One's commercial activity should therefore be motivated by a spiritual purpose, [for example,] the refinement [of the

---

108. [See *Shabbos* 31a, *Tur* and *Shulchan Aruch, Orach Chayim* 156.]
109. *[Tehillim* 15:2.]
110. *Makkos* 24a.
111. [*Shmos* 20:9; ibid. 34:21.]
112. [*Devarim* 16:18.]
113. [See *Likkutei Torah, Parshas Teitzei* 37a ff.; the *maamar* known as *Ve-Yadaata* (Moscow) 5656, in *Sefer HaMaamarim* 5657, p. 56ff.; and elsewhere.]
114. [*Yeshayahu* 45:12.]
115. [*Mikdash Melech* on *Zohar* I, 205b.]

material substance of the world] which is achieved through this activity.

Accordingly, when one asks G-d for help in earning a livelihood one must first be certain that his business constitutes a pure medium. Furthermore, one should ensure that this business is a vessel fit to receive blessings, i.e., that it is conducted according to [G-d's] intent. Nevertheless, since faith transcends [the level of our conscious processes], a person [often] does not pay attention to the above [concepts in his day-to-day functioning].

Thus we can understand what it means to "nourish faith"[116] — to cause it to radiate within ourselves [i.e., to internalize this potential and bring our faith within our intellectual grasp]. This was the spiritual task of Moshe, the shepherd who nurtured faith, allowing "the righteous" [i.e., every individual among the Jewish people] to "live by his faith,"[117] so that it is felt with an inward vitality.

Moshe [has the potential to nurture the faith of the Jewish people] because he draws down the attribute of *Daas* ("knowledge" or "understanding") into their souls.[118] [Furthermore, his efforts are not directed only to the upper echelons of the people. Rather, as implied by the verse,[119]] "I shall grant pasture in your fields for your animals," [he also] drew down the attribute of *Daas* to [the common people, those whose] souls [can be described as] "brutish".[120]

---

116. [See ch. 4, above.]
117. *[Chavakuk 2:4.]*
118. See *Torah Or,* beginning of *Parshas Mishpatim; Toras Chayim* [on that *parshah*]; and other sources.
119. *[Devarim 11:15.]*
120. *[Yirmeyahu 31:26.]*

Daas is live feeling. Moshe, the shepherd of faith, nourishes the faith in the souls of the Jewish people, causing it to be experienced with inner feeling.

Synopsis

Everyone can find examples of the above-described paradox in his own conduct when he asks G-d for something that contradicts His will. People often err in their self-appraisal, considering that they are worthy of children, wealth and esteem, and forgetting that even if they have not committed gross sins, there are many subtler faults that ought to be considered, such as the manner and the mediums through which one earns a livelihood. [Such anomalies may be averted by internalizing one's faith.]

"Nourishing" faith means causing it to radiate and be thoroughly integrated within oneself.

XII

This, then, is what is meant by the verse, "Your nation are all righteous": G-d's people, who are born in holiness and purity as prescribed by the Torah, are all righteous when we look at the source of their souls. [This quality is reflected] in our faith, the faith of the entire Jewish people, in "the One G-d."

All Jews declare, "Hear O Israel, G-d is our L-rd, G-d is one," and "Blessed be the Name of His glorious kingdom forever and ever." These two verses reflect our faithful acceptance of the two [manifestations of G-dliness], *memaleh kol almin* and *sovev kol almin*. [This faith is the essence of our spiritual personalities.] The fundamental goal of our service of G-d is [to extend the scope of this potential], so that our faith will radiate within [our intellects, allowing for] a developed grasp [of both the concepts

— "Hear O Israel,...G-d is one," and "Blessed be the Name of His glorious kingdom forever and ever"] — to the point that it is experienced and internalized.

[Meditation on the phrase,] "Blessed be the Name of His glorious Kingdom," requires] that one should systematically contemplate the unique nature of creation *yesh me'ayin* (lit., "something from nothing"; i.e., creation *ex nihilo*), and the wondrous manner in which it is brought about.

[To explain:] The Divine [light which we call] *ayin* must be close to the *yesh,* the entity being created, [to bring it into being]. [Since the Divine light is enclothed within the created beings themselves, it must "descend" — i.e., progressively obscure itself — to a level at which it shares a commonalty with them.] Indeed, it is for this purpose that it is obliged to undergo the entire *Seder HaHishtalshelus,* [the chainlike system of descent whereby successively less-spiritual worlds come into being], in order to bring the Divine *ayin* close [to the level of created beings] and thus bring them into existence.

[Conversely, at the very same time,] the Creator must conceal Himself from created beings, [for were His presence to be openly revealed, it would be impossible for a created thing to perceive itself to be an entity with an independent existence. The fusion of G-d's closeness and distance] in the creation and the wondrous [process this involves] are explained at length in other sources.[121]

Similarly, [one should meditate on] how no entity can live independently of the Divine life-force that animates it. This should be grasped with inner feeling to the extent that just as a person feels that he is alive, he should feel that the world is alive, animated by a G-dly life-force. When he feels within his soul that the world lives with Divine life, he will

---

121. [*Sefer HaMaamarim 5677,* p. 62, *Sefer HaMaamarim — Kuntreisim,* Vol. II, p. 278b; see also *Shaar HaYichud VehaEmunah, passim.*]

feel the Divine life-force and not material substance (*yesh*). And with this he will have fulfilled what G-d desired of him.

Similarly, when one meditates on the phrase, "G-d is one," he should grasp the concept of G-d's oneness as firmly as if he saw it [with his own eyes], [and appreciated] the various dimensions of this oneness. This involves meditation on how "before Him, everything is of no significance"; i.e., in relation to the *Or Ein Sof,* the Infinite Light, the worlds are of no account whatever. The degree of *bittul* [that results from such an awareness] is *bittul bimetzius,* utter and complete self-effacement.

To illustrate [this concept] with an analogy. In comparison to a sage of sublime and unique wisdom, a man of moderate gifts is of no significance at all. The illustrious sage does not consider the latter's wisdom to be inferior wisdom, but plain foolishness. In fact he sees no difference between the man of lesser wisdom and an outright fool. Of King Shlomo, for example, it is written, "And G-d granted wisdom to Shlomo."[122] So richly was he thus endowed that by comparison the wisdom of lesser men may be considered mere foolishness. How much more so can a person who is not wise be considered a fool. Indeed, relative to a true sage, a person lacking in understanding may appear to be barely human.

[The way in which a sage is distant from others does not stem from pride or conceit. It is not that he looks down on others: he is simply on a higher level of understanding. Just as people in two different geographic locations may not be aware of each other's existence, the sage is simply in a different realm and cannot share his wisdom with others who are not on his level.]

---

122. [*I Melachim* 5:26.]

Synopsis

[The internalization of faith involves integrating one's faith within the context of one's intellectual faculties.] In regard to [the light of] *memaleh kol almin*, faith shines within one's meditation on the nature of creation *yesh me'ayin*. This involves [comprehension of] the [simultaneous] closeness and concealment [that characterizes the relationship between] the *yesh* and the *ayin*.

In regard to [the light of] *sovev kol almin*, [faith] shines within one's meditation on [the concept that] "G-d is one." An awareness of this brings created beings to a state of *bittul*, of utter insignificance. This is illustrated by the analogy of a moderately wise man who is not considered as wise at all when compared to an illustrious sage whose wisdom is of his essence.

XIII

The spiritual analog to the above can be understood in regard to the utter insignificance of the entire concept of [separate] existence. Just as the superlative gifts of an outstanding sage cause him to regard the wisdom of a mediocrity not as an inferior degree of wisdom but rather as the very opposite of wisdom, similarly, because of the awesomely wondrous nature of the *Or Ein Sof*, the Infinite Light, and its utter transcendence [of the concept] of separate existence, the existence of the world is as nothing.

There is, however, a difference in this regard between the higher [i.e., more spiritual] worlds and the lower worlds. The higher worlds appreciate their insignificance in relation to [G-d's] essence; i.e., they know and appreciate the transcendence of the *Or Ein Sof* and [perceive] how [in comparison with it] the worlds are of no significance whatsoever. This knowledge and perception itself causes them to transcend their individual existence, [i.e., to lose all sense of independent identity and lose all self-concern].

[This feeling can also be understood within the above] analogy. When a man of lesser wisdom acknowledges his inferiority relative to an illustrious sage, his self-nullification affects the very essence of his being. Everyone foregoes his self-assertion before a sage of truly great stature. This includes even simple people who have no appreciation of his great wisdom. Their self-annulment is, however, of an entirely different nature. We observe that they draw close to the sage and desire to serve him, attaching self-importance to the fact that they share a connection with him.

In contrast, someone who does appreciate wisdom, though he be incomparably inferior to the towering sage, refrains from drawing close to him. On the contrary, the very essence of his being is overcome by self-nullification.

Thus, though both kinds of people sense their own nothingness relative to the gifted sage, the nature of their self-nullification differs. In a wise man of a lesser stature this awareness permeates his entire being, [so that he loses all self-concern — a level comparable to the *bittul bimetzius* of the spiritual realms. In contrast,] the very *bittul* of a simple person causes him [paradoxically] to rise in self-esteem.

The analog to these concepts can be understood regarding the difference between the self-effacement (*bittul*) of the higher worlds, [which is complete and total] like the self-effacement of the lesser sage, and the self-effacement of these lower worlds, which resembles that of the simple person whose self-esteem is [not shaken — indeed it is enhanced — by his connection with a sage], even though in truth this self-esteem is unwarranted.

Synopsis

Relative to a ray of *Or Ein Sof,* the Infinite Light, the existence of this world is utterly of no consequence.

An analogy is drawn between the *bittul* of the spiritual worlds and the utter self-nullification of a minor sage in the presence of a sage in whom wisdom is of his very essence. By contrast, the *bittul* of [our] lowly material world can be compared to the *bittul* of a simple person to such a sage, for through his connection with the sage, the simple person's self-esteem in fact grows.

XIV

Let us now focus on the concept of [how our existence] has no real significance; i.e., how an entity, though a non-being, can nevertheless continue to exist. [This is the nature of the relationship between the light of *sovev kol almin* and the lower levels of existence: although these lower levels of being do exist, "everything before You is of no significance."]

[To explain this concept by extending the above analogy to a familiar situation] in the service [of G-d] and the observance of the Torah and its *mitzvos:* There are some people who are innately attracted to Torah study, and would dearly love to see [their] children and grandchildren involved in it. They are drawn towards the students of Torah, develop a connection with them, and have an active sensitivity to all holy matters. Nevertheless, their closeness is not entirely genuine.

Why is this? — Because of peer influence; their environment prevents them from really drawing close [to the Torah]. [A person in such a predicament is apprehensive in case making such a commitment] would be considered socially inappropriate. In the Yiddish idiom, *es past im nit*. If he were to participate regularly in a communal study session, enroll his son in a *cheder* or in a *yeshivah*, or establish a genuine and open connection with G-d-fearing people, his social circle might raise an eyebrow of disapproval.

Similarly, there are people who are committed to the service of G-d but who are hindered in [their study of] Torah and, in particular, in the "service of the heart," i.e., in prayer,[123] by [their relations with] others. These hindrances vary according to the nature of the individuals involved and according to the circumstances of time and place, and sometimes must even be fought off.

Nevertheless, in a moment of truth — i.e., when a person meditates on the real purpose for which he was created, on the final goal of all his efforts, and the Divine intent for which he was granted children and grandchildren — he will understand that the ultimate end of all these facets of his life is the fulfillment of the Creator's will and His intent. [A person who has attained this realization will not at all be affected by other people.]

The same applies to those whose service of G-d in Torah study and prayer stems from the core of truth in their souls, i.e., those whose service of G-d endows them with an internalized awareness of the truth. Such people are not disturbed by others at all. For example, in times of Divine favor on Rosh HaShanah or Yom Kippur, or when serving G-d through joy on Simchas Torah, such a person will not at all be disturbed by other people. It is not that he makes a point of considering them to be less worthy than himself; rather, he [will simply continue with his own service,] without paying any attention to them whatsoever because, [at this time,] their presence is of no consequence to him.

---

123. [See *Sifri, Ekev* 11:13; *Taanis* 2a.]

Although at an earlier stage he could have been distracted by people of comparable level, now that his own efforts have brought him to an internalized awareness of the truth, he is involved with himself and cannot be affected by them. [At this level of awareness,] the presence of others is totally of no account. Just as the inhabitants of another city do not affect him, so too, when one internalizes his awareness of the truth, he is in a different place entirely and others do not disturb him. Indeed, confronting him they cease to assert themselves. As the popular adage goes, "No one can resist the truth."

The analog to this model exists in the spiritual realms. The *Or Ein Sof,* the Infinite Light, transcends the created worlds entirely, to the extent that relative to it they are entirely insignificant, as if they did not exist at all. This is the meaning of the verse, "Hear O Israel... G-d is one." And our meditation on the oneness of G-d can lead to a thorough comprehension [and application of this level of complete *bittul*].

Synopsis

As an analogy to illustrate how [the worlds] are of no significance at all, it is explained that there are people who are attracted and draw close to Torah scholars, but [hesitate to make a genuine commitment because] they are uneasy about facing their peers. Similarly, there are people who serve G-d, and yet they feel inhibited by those around them. Nevertheless, at a time of [Divine] favor, other people do not deflect them from their path, because they have been elevated to a level at which the presence of others is meaningless to them. [Similarly, the light of *sovev kol almin* utterly transcends all other existence, to the extent that "Everything before Him is of no significance."]

XV

We can now understand the meaning of the verse, "And you shall command [the Children of Israel]."[124] [As explained above, based on the connection between the words *tzavta* ("connection") and *tzivui* ("command"), this charge can be interpreted as a directive for Moshe Rabbeinu to establish a bond with the Jewish people. This, in turn] allows him to connect the souls of Israel [to their Source].

When this is accomplished, "they will bring you olive oil." [To explain:] Moshe endows the souls of the Jewish people with the strength to reveal the superiority of the [seemingly lowest levels of the individual soul and of the Jewish people as a whole, known metaphorically as] the "foot", as explained above.[125] [In particular, his influence brings to the surface the power of *mesirus nefesh* that is latent within every Jew.]

There is an extension of Moshe in every generation[126] who serves as a "shepherd of faith," [nourishing and] strengthening the faith [of the Jewish people *in every generation*], enabling "the righteous [to] live by his faith," with an inner vitality. Moreover, by virtue of Moshe's influence, "Your nation are all righteous..., they are the branch of My planting." This refers to *tinokos shel beis rabban,* Jewish children who study the Torah. The potential [for these expressions of our fundamental Jewish essence] is also actualized by "the faithful shepherd," the leaders of the Jewish people who invigorate their souls and strengthen their faith.

In particular, this is expressed in the time of exile, in eras such as the time of Haman, who arose to destroy us, heaven forbid. Mordechai, who was equivalent to Moshe,

---

124. [The queries raised in chs. 3 and 4 above are now to be resolved.]
125. [Cf. chs. 5 and 6 above.]
126. [Cf. ch. 4 above.]

arose at that time to strengthen our faith and [rally us] to stand fast in the study of the Torah. Haman sought to kill and exterminate the entire Jewish people, and said, "I will begin by striking at these children." Significantly, it was precisely the *tinokos shel beis rabban* whom Mordechai [gathered together] for communal study, and it was [through their merit] that the "enemy and the avenger" were silenced.[127]

[These insights can grant us a fresh understanding of a verse quoted above, concerning which a number of queries were posed.[128] In the first instance, that verse specified that the olives for the *Menorah* had to be] "crushed for the light." In the time of exile, everyone is broken and crushed — but it is precisely at such a time that one reaches the [essence of the] luminary itself. This in turn allows us "to keep a constant light burning." For this alludes to [the light within the soul of every one of us, as it is written],[129] "The soul of man is a lamp of G-d." This light refers to the Divine Name *Havayah* as it is manifest in the [Jewish] soul. When this dimension of the soul is revealed, i.e., when "*Havayah* is with him,"[130] then "the *Halachah* follows him in every instance."[131] I.e., the providence [G-d manifests] in the midst of nature [reflects and] reveals that which transcends nature. [Thus, although exile overtly represents a descent, it evokes an intense commitment on the part of the Jewish people which, in turn, brings about the revelation of transcendent G-dliness.]

We may now more fully understand the statement that "the Jews accepted what they had already begun,"[132] [i.e.,

---

127. [Cf. ch. 2 above.]
128. [Cf. ch. 3 above.]
129. *[Mishlei* 20:27.]
130. *[I Shmuel* 16:18.]
131. *Sanhedrin* 93b.
132. [The following passage summarizes the dominant theme of the *maamar*; cf. chs. 1 and 2 above.]

that the service of G-d described in the Purim narrative completed the process of accepting the Torah]. At the Giving of the Torah, [G-d] "held the mountain over them like a tub," [forcing them as it were to accept the Torah,] by revealing [G-dliness from above]. In contrast, in the time of exile, in the time of what "came to pass in the days of Achashverosh," [there was no revelation from above, and the Jews had to develop their connection with G-d through their own commitment].

[The setting for the Purim narrative] resembled what "came to pass in the days of Achaz." Achaz had "locked all the synagogues and houses of study" in order (heaven forbid) to sever the people's connection with G-d. This he began [by disrupting the study of] *tinokos shel beis rabban*. [At that time,] Yeshayahu [the prophet] challenged him: "What success will you have?" For ultimately, "Behold, I and the children whom G-d has given me as signs and wonders in Israel" [will prevent that from happening]. And, in fact, they reconstructed what Achaz had destroyed.

The situation was similar in the time of Haman. He conspired (heaven forbid) to destroy the Jewish people entirely, and likewise began by striking at the *tinokos shel beis rabban*. The response of Mordechai, the extension of Moshe in his generation, was to arise and gather together groups of people [for communal study of the Torah], strengthening their faith in G-d through the study of *tinokos shel beis rabban* — for this is the foundation, essence and root of the entire [Jewish people].

It was this initiative that represented "the affirmation" through actual *mesirus nefesh* "of what they had already begun." This indeed is the ultimate purpose of the exile — that [the Jewish people] should stand firm in the face of all the challenges that confront them, [and thus reveal their essential bond with G-d].

In this light we can understand the above-quoted passage: "And since that hour *I have hoped for Him,* for it is written, '[The Torah] will not be forgotten from the mouths of his descendants.'" It is precisely in the time of exile — when "darkness covers the earth," [as the Divine light is obscured] in a manifold sequence of concealments and veilings that create formidable hindrances and obstacles — that the power is granted from Above to transform the pervading darkness into "the light which is good,"¹³³ with children and grandchildren occupied in the [study of] Torah.

This, then, represents the explanation of the verse, "The Jews accepted what they had already begun." Through their endeavors with the *tinokos shel beis rabban,* the Jews of that time confirmed with actual *mesirus nefesh* the [spiritual commitment] they had begun when the Torah was given. And through this, they were found worthy of redemption.

Synopsis

The *maamar* explains how the extension of Moshe [in every generation] fortifies the faith [of his contemporaries], enabling it to illuminate them from within. In times of exile and of anti-Semitic edicts everyone is broken and battered — "crushed," [like the olives used for oil in the Sanctuary]. [However,] it is through this that one can make contact with the luminary itself, with the "soul of man [which] is a lamp of G-d."

The salvation of the Jewish people is brought about by *tinokos shel beis rabban* and by study of the Torah in public. During times of exile the Jewish people are granted the strength required for self-sacrificing endeavors for the fulfillment of the Torah

---

133. [Cf. *Bereishis* 1:4.]

and its commandments. It is through this self-sacrifice that they are found worthy of redemption.

Maamar מאמר
Yehi Havayah יהי הוי-ה
Elokeinu Imanu אלוקינו עמנו
5687 [1927]] תרפ״ז

"MAY THE L-RD OUR G-D BE WITH US
AS HE WAS WITH OUR FATHERS…"

[On Sunday, the third of Tammuz, having just been released from incarceration and capital sentence in Leningrad, the Rebbe Rayatz stood on the step of the train that was to take him to Kostroma, the city to which he had been exiled. He turned to the many chassidim who accompanied him to the station and, in the course of his farewell blessings, said loudly and clearly:[1]]

We ask G-d, blessed be He:[2] "May the L-rd our G-d be with us" — *and He will indeed be with us* — "as He was with our fathers; may He not forsake us, nor abandon us."[3]

We cannot be compared to our fathers, for they were characterized by *mesirus nefesh* — literal self-sacrifice — for the Torah and its *mitzvos*. This is reflected in the well-

---

1. [There are two versions of this text. One was published in *Sefer HaMaamarim 5687*, p. 195 ff., based on the manuscript of the Rebbe Rayatz; the other appeared in *Sefer HaMaamarim — Kuntreisim*, Vol. I, pp. 350-351, after being edited by him.

    The latter source, in which this text was originally published, states that it was recorded by one of the listeners. In fact, however, the text was prepared by the Rebbe Rayatz himself, who desired that it appear as listener's notes, rather than as his own words. (See *Likkutei Sichos*, Vol. XXIII, p. 158, footnote 13.)

    In the Table of Contents of *Sefer HaMaamarim 5687*, this text is listed under the heading of *Maamarim*, where it belongs thematically and chronologically. Strictly speaking, though, as the Rebbe points out in a footnote there, it is not a formal *maamar*, but an inspirational address. In the body of the text, moreover, the heading dates it six days late: "*Shabbos Parshas Balak*, 5687 [1927], in the city of my exile, Kostroma" — evidently out of deference to the convention according to which *maamarim* were traditionally delivered on a *Shabbos* or other festive date.]

2. [This opening phrase is found in the version of the text that appears in *Sefer HaMaamarim — Kuntreisim*, but not in the more formally-presented version appearing in *Sefer Maamarim 5687*.]

3. [In the original, יהי הוי-ה אלקינו עמנו, כאשר הי-ה עם אבותינו, אל יעזבנו ואל יטשנו; *I Melachim* 8:57.]

known statement of one of our holy forebears[4] (when the former regime tried to force the rabbis to institute reforms in Jewish education and in the status of rabbis and the rabbinate):

> Nevertheless, all the nations on the face of the earth must know: Our bodies alone were banished into exile to be ruled by the nations of the world. Our souls were never exiled, nor were they subjected to the rule of the nations.
>
> We must openly declare for all to hear, that with regard to everything involving our religion — the Torah of the people of Israel, with its commandments and customs — no one is going to impose his views on us,[5] and no force has the right to subjugate us.
>
> With all the power of Jewish stubbornness and with our thousand-year heritage of *mesirus nefesh*,[6] we

---

4. [The Rebbe Rashab. For partial paraphrases of the above statement, see: *Igros HaKodesh* (Letters) of the Rebbe Rayatz, Vol. I, p. 249, and Vol. IX, p. 428; *Sefer HaSichos 5702*, p. 111; *Sefer HaSichos 5705*, p. 29.

    Sefer HaSichos — *Toras Shalom* (p. 221, footnote 6) describes the stance taken by the Rebbe Rashab at the 1910 Petersburg Conference alluded to above. Stolypin, the Minister of the Interior, had threatened there that if his demands for reform were not met he would initiate pogroms throughout Russia. In response, the Rebbe Rashab addressed the above-quoted speech to the rabbinic leaders present, and concluded: "Our strength is the strength of the Torah: we have no other strength.... Fellow Jews: Do not desecrate the Name of Heaven! *Sanctify* the Name of Heaven!"

    There was an immediate uproar — but the assemblage voted to defy Stolypin.]

5. [See also the *maamar* entitled *Ki Li Bnei Yisrael 5687* (in *Sefer HaMaamarim 5687*, p. 182).]

6. [The version published in *Sefer HaMaamarim 5687* reads: "with the thousand-year heritage of Jewish fortitude...."]

must say, "Do not touch My anointed ones, and do not harm My prophets."[7]

This is the way a Jew permeated by *mesirus nefesh* spoke, whereas we do not have [even] the resolute strength to make a clear statement to the world and show what the wanton deeds of several hundred reckless Jewish youth are doing to Jews and to Jewish life. Everyone knows that the laws [of the Russian government] permit us to study the Torah and observe its *mitzvos* (albeit with certain limitations). It is betrayal and libel [on the part of these youths] that is leading us to prisons and hard-labor camps.

This is our request to G-d: "May He not forsake us, nor abandon us." May G-d give us the necessary fortitude not to be affected by physical suffering and, on the contrary, to accept it with joy.[8] The punishment which we must suffer (G-d forbid) for maintaining a *cheder,* for studying the Torah, or for observing its *mitzvos,* should reinforce us in the sacred task of strengthening Jewish life.

We must always bear in mind that prisons and hard-labor camps are transient, whereas the Torah, its *mitzvos,* and the Jewish people, are eternal.

May you all be strong and healthy, both materially and spiritually. I hope to G-d that the punishment which I must temporarily suffer will, with G-d's help, inject fresh vigor in [our] eternal [mission of] strengthening Jewish life, and that we will merit the fulfillment [of the promise] that "the L-rd our G-d [will] be with us as He was with our fathers," and that all of the Children of Israel will have light in their dwellings,[9] in both a spiritual and material sense.

---

7. [*Tehillim* 105:15; *I Divrei HaYamim* 16:22. In *Shabbos* 119b, the *Gemara* understands this verse as a charge not to disrupt the Torah study of schoolchildren or of adult scholars.]
8. [Cf. *Berachos* 60b; see also *Tanya,* ch. 26. In the version published in *Sefer HaMaamarim 5687,* this last phrase is omitted.]
9. [Cf. *Shmos* 10:23.]

Maamar
Havayah Li BeOzrai
5687 [1927]

מאמר
הוי-ה לי בעוזרי
תרפ"ז

"G-D IS AMONG THOSE WHO HELP ME..."

[This *maamar* was delivered on Tuesday, the twelfth of Tammuz, the date on which the Rebbe Rayatz was informed of his impending release from exile in Kostroma, and which is celebrated to this day as *Yud-Beis Tammuz, Chag HaGeulah* – the Festival of Liberation.]

I

"G-d is among those who help me; may I witness [the downfall of] those who hate me."[1] The wording here is problematic, appearing to imply that a person has many helpers, and that G-d is [merely] one of them. In truth, however,[2] "There is none else apart from Him." He alone, blessed be He, is the Creator Who brings a man into existence and animates him, and assists him in all his affairs. As *Rambam* declares:[3] "The foundation of all foundations and the pillar of all wisdom is to know that there exists a Prime Being, and He brings into existence every existing thing; and all things that exist in the heavens and earth and between them exist only by virtue of His true existence." Significantly, the initials of the first four Hebrew words of this passage (יסוד היסודות ועמוד החכמות) — "The foundation of all foundations and the pillar of all wisdom") spell the [transcendent] Divine Name *Havayah*.[4]

In this context, *echad* ("one") means *yachid* ("unique"). The term *echad* is nevertheless used in order to show that

---

1. [In the original, הוי-ה לי בעוזרי, ואני אראה בשונאי; *Tehillim* 118:7. In *Likkutei Sichos*, Vol. XXVIII, p. 149ff., the Rebbe explains why the Rebbe Rayatz based the *maamar* on this verse.]
2. [In the original, אין עוד מלבדו; *Devarim* 4:35.]
3. [In the original, יסוד היסודות ועמוד החכמות לידע שיש שם מצוי ראשון, והוא ממציא כל נמצא; *Hilchos Yesodei HaTorah* 1:1.]
4. [The term *Havayah* is a rearrangement of the letters of the Name י-ה-ו-ה which, out of deference to its sanctity, is not pronounced as written.]

"*Havayah* and *Elokim* are all one";[5] i.e., everything that has been created and brought into being is at one, in complete unity, with Him, for He is [an indivisible] unity. We, the entire Jewish people, believe with simple faith in the absolute truth that all the life-energy of created beings, their existence, and any salvation that comes to them, derives only from G-d. As it is written,[6] "He stands at the right side of the pauper to save him from those who condemn his soul."

This relates especially to someone who is broken and crushed by extensive suffering, heaven forbid. This is reflected in the verse,[7] "The offering [desirable] to G-d is a contrite spirit, a crushed and broken heart..." Likewise, the *Zohar*[8] teaches that "G-d is served with broken vessels." For a person who is broken and contrite is self-effacing and humble in his own eyes, and this makes him a fit vessel for G-dliness.

A person who sees himself as a self-sufficient [and important] entity, a *yesh*, is not a vessel for G-dliness. Our Sages teach[9] that [with regard to a haughty person, G-d says]: "He and I cannot dwell [together]." By contrast, with regard to a person who holds himself humble — particularly after his soul has experienced the bitter taste of contrition and he has turned to G-d with all his heart and all his might — it is written,[10] "I dwell on high, in a holy place, yet [also] with him who is contrite and humble of spirit."

Accordingly, it is difficult to understand the phrase, "G-d is among those who help me," for it implies that G-d

---

5. [*Zohar* II, 26b.]
6. [*Tehillim* 109:31.]
7. [*Tehillim* 51:19.]
8. [II, 86b; III, 9a.]
9. [*Sotah* 5a.]
10. [*Yeshayahu* 57:15.]

is one helper in partnership with others. We must therefore understand: Who are those who help others, particularly in a time of distress, heaven forbid?

In practice, we see the opposite. Most people who follow their natural habit draw close to those who are successful ("A wealthy man has many friends"[11]), and keep their distance from those whose days are tough and whose spirits are embittered, heaven forbid. Who, then, are those who help a person? For the verse implies that a person has true helpers, among whom G-d is to be found.

Also requiring explanation is [King David's] request, "May I witness [the downfall of] those who hate me." Seemingly, it would have been more appropriate for him to have asked that his enemies and haters be transformed into friends and intimates. It is true that David's enmity was directed only to those hate G-d; as it is written,[12] "G-d, do I not hate those who hate You? And against those who rise against You, do I not strive?" Nevertheless, on the verse,[13] "May sinners (חטאים) cease from the earth," our Sages note that the wording of the Hebrew implies,[14] "May *sins* cease" and not "May sinners cease." Seen in this light, the verse requests that sinners should turn to G-d in *teshuvah*. A desire to "witness [the downfall of] those who hate me" thus raises difficulties.

The intent of [David's] statement becomes even more problematic when one considers that [when cursed by Shimi ben Gera] David himself [counseled restraint], saying,[15] "For G-d has told him to curse... Who then shall say,

---

11. [Cf. *Mishlei* 14:20.]
12. [*Tehillim* 139:21.]
13. [*Tehillim* 104:35.]
14. [On the non-literal level of *derush*, reading the initial letter *ches* of חטאים as if it were vocalized with a *chataf patach* instead of with a *patach*; see *Berachos* 10a, and *Rashi* there.]
15. [*II Shmuel* 16:10. See also *Tanya — Iggeres HaKodesh*, Epistle 25, in *Lessons In Tanya*, Vol. V, pp. 80-82.]

'Why have you done this?'" [Our verse seems to indicate a very different approach. Moreover, David's] foes [thus] included individuals who were nurtured by holy sources. Further examples are Doeg and Achitofel (as mentioned in chs. 52 and 55 of *Tehillim*), who outwardly conducted themselves according to the laws of the Torah. If so, the [request to] "witness [the downfall of] those who hate me" appears to be [a request for] vengeance, which in any possible form is an undesirable trait. How could David make such a request?

Another point: What is the apparent connection between the two clauses of our verse? It appears that it is *because* "G-d is among those who help me" that "I [will] witness [the downfall of] those who hate me." This seems to imply that witnessing the downfall of one's foes becomes possible when a person has helpers with whom G-d joins, as it were.

II

These concepts can be understood [by prefacing] the explanation of our Sages' statement,[16] — הבא לטהר מסייעין לו — "A person who comes to purify [himself] is granted assistance." [Here also] the Hebrew term for "is granted assistance" uses a plural form, whereas [as above] the sole helper is the Holy One, blessed be He.

The infinitive לטהר is also problematic. This is a transitive verb, implying that one also intends to purify others. Seemingly, the intransitive verb ליטהר would have been more appropriate, for this would imply that the individual himself desires to become pure, rather than to purify others.

The above concepts may be clarified in light of the verse,[17] "Your statutes were my songs when I dwelled in

---

16. [*Shabbos* 104a.]
17. [*Tehillim* 119:54.]

fear." On these words our Sages teach[18] that [G-d exclaimed], "David! You call them songs?!" — and David was punished for this.

[What is the meaning of this passage?] David was extolling the Torah, in that the life-energy and continuing existence of the world depends on the meticulous observance of any of its *mitzvos*. For the creation of the world came about through the medium of the Torah, which testifies concerning itself,[19] "I was the implement with which the Holy One, blessed be He, [created the world]." Similarly, the *Zohar* states,[20] "The Holy One, blessed be He, looked into the Torah and created the world."

The continued existence of the entire world thus depends on the Torah, as indicated by our Sages' statement,[21] "The Holy One, blessed be He, made a condition with all the works of Creation: If Israel accepts the Torah, you will continue to exist; if not, I shall return you all to nothingness and void."

Thus, when people are involved in the Torah and its study, particularly in communal study, additional [G-dly] light and revelation are drawn down within the worlds. Similarly, by means of the sacrifices, [all] the worlds are elevated to higher levels; as is stated [in the *Zohar*[22]], "The secret of the sacrifices ascends to the secret of the *Ein Sof*," G-d's infinity. For the Hebrew term for "sacrifice" (קרבן) is related to קירוב, meaning "to come close." Thus the phrase,[23] "When a person shall sacrifice...," can be interpreted to mean, "When a person wishes to draw close to G-dliness...."

---

18. [*Sotah* 35a; see also *Tanya — Kuntres Acharon,* Essay Six, in *Lessons In Tanya,* Vol. V, p. 365ff.]
19. [*Bereishis Rabbah* 1:1.]
20. [II, 161b.]
21. [*Shmos Rabbah* 21:6.]
22. [II, 239a; III 26b.]
23. [*Vayikra* 1:2, interpreted in *Likkutei Torah,* and in the *maamar* entitled *Basi LeGani 5710* (English translation; Kehot, N.Y., 5750).]

And the verse continues, "...of you an offering," which indicates that drawing close to G-d depends on one's own divine service. As [Rabbeinu] Bachye explains,[24] a sacrifice involves drawing close [Divine] powers and the [influences conveyed by G-d's] Names. And it is well known that every elevation[25] [of the world through our divine service] elicits a downward flow[26] of Divine influence.

The additional [Divine] light and life-energy that is drawn down into the worlds through the sacrifices underlies their description as[27] "a pleasing fragrance to G-d — a pleasure which generates a downward flow of spiritual light to the level of the Name *Havayah,* and [subsequently] to the various created worlds.

In the era of the *Beis HaMikdash,* Divinity[28] was overtly apparent. Thus, for example, there were ten miracles which took place in the *Beis HaMikdash.*[29] So, too, [at each of the three Pilgrim Festivals],[30] "Just as a person would come to *be seen* [before G-d, as the Torah requires], so too, he would come to *see* [Divinity]." For in the *[Beis Ha]Mikdash* one could actually see G-dly light revealed.

This was especially apparent within the Holy of Holies, where the *Or Ein Sof,* the infinity of G-d's light, would openly radiate. As a [spatial] expression of this,[31] "The space occupied by the Ark was not included in the measure." [Though there were ten cubits from the Ark to the northern wall, ten cubits from the Ark to the southern wall, and the Ark itself was two-and-a-half cubits long, the total distance from wall to wall remained twenty cubits.]

---

24. [On *Vayikra* 1:9.]
25. [In the original, *haalaah.*]
26. [In the original, *hamshachah.*]
27. *[Vayikra* 1:9.]
28. [In the original, *Elokus.*]
29. *[Avos* 5:4.]
30. *[Chagigah* 2a.]
31. *[Yoma* 21a.]

What is most striking about this phenomenon is that all the items in the *[Beis Ha]Mikdash* are required to be precise with regard to time, space, dimensions and weight; indeed, altering a dimension invalidates the object in question. Nevertheless, [with regard to the Ark,] the space itself did not occupy space. This [transcendence of space] was an expression of the overt illumination of the infinite dimension of the *Or Ein Sof.*

All these [revelations] came about by means of the sacrifices — provided that they were offered according to the laws of the Torah. If there was any disqualifying factor whatever, the entire sequence of elevation[25] [of worldliness] and [the consequent] downward flow[26] of light was nullified.

To cite a parallel: When one wears *tefillin*, the [Supernal] intellective attributes known as *Mochin* are drawn down into *Z'eir Anpin* [which is a level of Divinity corresponding to the emotive attributes, or *middos*, of mortals]. For the four Scriptural passages contained in the *tefillin* represent the four *Mochin*. Thus, the wearing of *tefillin* augments the downward flow of G-dly light into the world.

[To explain:] The creation of the world has its source in the *Middos*, [the Supernal] emotive attributes. This is alluded to in the verse,[32] "[In] six days, G-d created the heavens and the earth." [The verse does not state בששת, meaning "In six days," but rather ששת, literally meaning "six days." The Sages of the Kabbalah explain that] the six days refer to the six Supernal emotive attributes, [which are the source for the world's existence].

---

32. [Shmos 20:11.]

Similarly, [the connection between the creation and the Supernal emotive attributes, or *Middos,* is reflected in] the verse,[33] "Remember Your mercies... and Your acts of kindness, for they are eternal." [The word מעולם, here translated as "eternal", also means "of the world."] This indicates that mercy, kindness, [and the other Supernal emotive attributes,] share a connection with the world. The Supernal intellectual attributes, by contrast, transcend any connection with our world.[34] [For intellect] in essence is a revelation for oneself, and there is a vast difference between a revelation for oneself and a revelation to another person, [the latter being an appropriate analogy for the relationship between our world and its G-dly Source].

Nevertheless, [notwithstanding the apparent distance between the *Mochin* and the lower levels of Divinity], through [the *mitzvah* of] *tefillin* the Supernal intellectual attributes are drawn down into *Z'eir Anpin,* and [thus] additional light is drawn down into the world. This applies only when the parchment, ink, writing, and fashioning of the *tefillin,* follow the dictates of Torah law. If, however, there is any disqualifying factor, the downward current [of Divine light] is negated.

The same applies with regard to all the *mitzvos.* When they are performed according to law, they serve as a medium to draw down additional [Divine] light and life-energy into the world.

III

To explain this concept: We find that G-d's commandments are known by various names — *eidos* (testimonials), *chukim* (statutes), and *mishpatim* (judgments). [The *eidos*

---

33. [*Tehillim* 25:6.]
34. [In the *maamar* entitled *Issa BeMidrash T[eh]illim 5653* (English translation; Sichos In English, 5753), these concepts are explained at length.]

include commandments] such as *Shabbos* which [the Torah describes[35] as] "a sign to the Children of Israel," and [dwelling in] *sukkos,* [of which it is written,[36]] "So that your [future] generations will know that I caused the Children of Israel to live in *sukkos* when I brought them out of the land of Egypt."

Mishpatim are those commandments that follow the dictates of reason, such as [the prohibitions against] robbery, theft, deceit, [the obligation to] honor one's parents, and the like. *Chukim* are [the commandments] that do not follow the dictates of reason, but are Scriptural decrees. As *Rashi* states (in his commentary on the verse [which introduces the commandment of the Red Heifer],[37] "This is the Torah's decree..."): "Satan and the gentile nations vex the Jewish people, saying, 'What does this *mitzvah* mean to you? What is its rationale?' The Torah therefore calls it a *chukah,* a decree issued by Me; you have no license to query it."

This is a person's [life-]task — that the fulfillment of the commandments whose [rationale can be] intellectually understood should be [motivated by the same] unquestioning commitment to G-d's will, the same *kabbalas ol,* as the commandments which are *chukim.* Even the commandments [whose rationale] can be grasped should not be fulfilled because we comprehend that rationale, but because they are G-d's *mitzvos,* as commanded by the Torah.

Similarly, with regard [to a man's conduct] in every element of his worldly affairs, he should always weigh and measure every move according to the standards of the Torah. [Even] activities which are neither forbidden nor [explicitly] permitted, i.e., they are left to our choice, or activities which mortal understanding would accept or even

---

35. [*Shmos* 31:17.]
36. [*Vayikra* 23:43.]
37. [*Bamidbar* 19:1.]

obligate, should not be undertaken unless one has first weighed them against the Torah's standards.

This concept is reflected in the blessing recited [after one has been called to the public Reading of the Torah, praising G-d][38] "Who gave us the Torah of truth and planted *eternal life* (חיי עולם) within us." [Since, as explained above, עולם means both "eternal" and "world", the blessing can be understood as speaking of guidance with regard to] "life within the world," conduct in the sphere of behavior that is left to our choice: here, too, our approval or disapproval should be determined by the Torah's standards. If a particular line of conduct will benefit or buttress the Torah, it should be encouraged. And if it could possibly lead to the opposite, or to a slackening of [adherence to] a *mitzvah* or custom, it should be rejected in all possible ways with *mesirus nefesh,* with self-sacrifice, even when mortal reason would accept or obligate it.

[An awareness of] the Torah's standards can be cultivated solely through a comprehension of the *pnimiyus* — the innermost, mystical dimension — of the Torah. This reflects the approach of David, of whom it is said,[39] וה׳-ה עמו — "G-d is with him." As understood by our Sages (*Sanhedrin* 93b), this means that "the *Halachah* follows his [rulings] at all times."

The intent can be explained as follows: It is written,[40] הליכות עולם לו — "The paths of the world are his." [Interpreting on the non-literal level of *derush,*] our Sages[41] [extend the meaning of the verse,] saying, "Do not read *halichos* ('the paths'); read *halachos* ('Torah laws')." [This implies that] through [the study of] *Halachah,* Torah law,

---

38. [*Siddur Tehillat HaShem,* p. 70.]
39. [*I Shmuel* 16:18. David's connection with the hidden dimension of the Torah becomes apparent later in the present chapter.]
40. [*Chavakuk* 3:6.]
41. [*Megillah* 28b.]

one will acquire "the paths of the world"; even within our material world G-dly light will manifestly shine.

[This is also indicated by a verse concerning Avraham Avinu:[42]] "For I have known him, for he commands his descendants and his household who follow him to observe the path of G-d *(Havayah),* to perform righteousness and judgment in the earth." [The use of the Name *Havayah* in the above verse is significant.] The world is brought into being [through the medium of] the Name *Elokim.* (This is reflected in the numerical equivalence *(gematria)* of *Elokim* (אלקים) and *hateva* (הטבע), which means "nature".) Serving G-d through the Torah and its commandments is intended to draw down the revelation of the Name *Havayah,* which transcends nature, [into our world which is governed by natural laws].

[The verse teaches that] "the path of *Havayah*" is reached by *tzedakah* [lit., "righteousness"; i.e., charity] that is regulated by *mishpat* ["judgment"]. This is also indicated by the verse,[43] "You established judgment and righteousness within Yaakov" [i.e., among the Jewish people]. Yishmael [also offers] kindness — but only after he has satisfied all his own needs to the point of luxury will he give charity to another.

The kindness of Avraham, by contrast, is subject to judgment: a Jew judges himself, providing for no more than his own necessities and giving his [remaining] resources to others. [Conduct of this nature] causes the [transcendent] Name *Havayah* to be revealed in the world. Seen in this light, the above teaching of the Sages, that "the *Halachah* follows [David's rulings] at all times," means that David elicited a revelation of the Name *Havayah* in this world. This is especially accomplished by disseminating Torah

---

42. [*Bereishis* 18:19.]
43. [*Tehillim* 99:4.]

through communal [study sessions]; as our Sages[44] comment on the verse,[45] "And You, G-d, protect them; shield them from this generation forever."

[On this basis, we can appreciate the uniqueness of King David's divine service.] Our Sages (*Eruvin* 53a) state: "David revealed the teachings (*galei masechta*); Shaul did not reveal the teachings." *Rashi* (commenting on *Gittin* 59a) explains that although Shaul was a great Torah scholar, he did not teach others. David, by contrast, revealed the teachings: he would labor in Torah study, and issue practical halachic directives.[46]

Perceived through the eyes of *Chassidus,* the meaning [of the phrase is expanded]. *[Masechta* ("the teachings") recalls *masach* ("veil").*]* When "revealing the teachings," David was "removing veils" of obscurity and uncovering the hidden [inner meanings of the Torah].

[For even the Torah is veiled.] Just as there is an Egypt, [a state of limitation,[47]] within the realm of evil, so, too, there is a [constraining] Egypt within the realm of holiness — namely, the fact that the Torah, which is G-d's [infinite] wisdom, has been garbed in terms conceivable by man's [finite] intelligence; for example,[48] "if Reuven would claim thus and Shimon thus, such and such should be the verdict

---

44. [The particular source intended is not noted in the *maamar*. The reference appears to be to the statement in *Vayikra Rabbah* 26:2 (and other sources) that the knowledge of the Torah was very widespread in David's age. He would pray that the wickedness of many of his contemporaries would not affect the righteous.]
45. [*Tehillim* 12:8.]
46. [Cf. *Rashi* on *Eruvin* 53a.]
47. [*Torah Or,* p. 71c, explains that the Hebrew name for Egypt, *Mitzrayim* (מצרים), is almost identical with the word *meitzarim* (מיצרים), which means straits or limitations. In chassidic thought, Egypt is thus more than a geographic location: it refers to all limitations on the essential G-dliness that permeates the world, the Torah, and our souls.*]*
48. [Cf. *Tanya,* ch. 5.]

between them." And this verdict can be understood even by mortal logic.

Thus there is a possibility for error. (As explained elsewhere:[49] If one studies the revealed dimension of Torah [law] alone, without also studying the *pnimiyus* of Torah or at least works of *Mussar,* one can forget the [Divine] Giver of the Torah. This can happen especially to those who pride themselves on their Torah [achievements]; they are punished by erring with regard to a explicit halachic ruling. Even more at risk are those whose scholarly contributions are original but unfounded.)

David, by contrast, studied the spiritual dimension of the laws, the profound mystical intentions illuminated by the *pnimiyus* of the Torah — a realm to which unaided mortal intellect has no access.

In this manner he "revealed the teachings," removing veils of obscurity to the extent that as a result of his efforts, even human intellect could actually appreciate Divinity as manifest on the worldly plane. In this spirit [he exclaims],[50] "How manifold are Your works, O G-d," and[51] "How great are Your works, O G-d."

Shaul, although he was a great Torah sage, sinned by following his reason.[52] David's divine service, by contrast, centered on *kabbalas ol,* an unquestioning acceptance of G-d's yoke. For this reason "G-d is with him," meaning that "the *Halachah* follows his [rulings] at all times" — for he drew down a revelation of the Name *Havayah* into our world.

---

49. [*Shulchan Aruch, Orach Chaim,* sec. 47, and commentary of *Bach; Kuntreis Etz Chaim,* pp. 42ff., 82ff.]
50. [*Tehillim* 104:24.]
51. [*Ibid.* 92:6.]
52. [See *I Shmuel,* ch. 15.]

IV

When David was in distress, forced to wander and flee from the pursuit of all the enemies who rose up against him, and when his material situation was unfavorable, he would rejoice in the Torah. Meditating on how the existence of all the worlds depends on the meticulous observance of any one of its *mitzvos*, he concluded that all worldly affairs are absolutely insignificant when compared to the Torah. Hence, his own material situation, too, was of no consequence whatever to him, because of the light of the Torah that shone within his soul. Indeed, the light of the *pnimiyus* of the Torah brought him great joy.

On this basis, we can appreciate the meaning of the verse cited above, "Your statutes were my songs when I dwelled in fear." [The word מגור has two meanings:] In addition to the meaning "sojourn", as in the verse,[53] "We came to sojourn (לגור) in the land," it also means "fear", as in the verses, "Do not fear (תגורו) any man,"[54] and "He saved me from all my fears (מגורותי).״[55]

[In David's instance, both meanings apply.] Throughout the entire time he was wandering and filled with fear because of his foes and pursuers, he derived his vitality and spiritual joy from the *pnimiyus* of the Torah. This is what he meant by the verse, "Your statutes were my songs (even) when I dwelled in fear."

If so, why was David punished for making such a statement? After all, it is explicitly written,[56] "[The Torah] is a tree of life for those who hold fast to it, and those who support it are happy." Why, then, was he punished?

---

53. [*Bereishis* 47:4.]
54. [*Devarim* 1:17.]
55. [*Tehillim* 34:5.]
56. [*Mishlei* 3:18.]

This concept can be understood by means of our Sages' interpretation of the verse,[57] "The blossoms can be seen in the land; the time of the singing bird has come, and the voice of the dove is heard in our land," *Midrash Rabbah*[58] teaches:

"'The blossoms can be seen in the land': This alludes to Mordechai and his company, and Ezra and his company....

'The time of the singing bird has come': The time has come for Israel to be redeemed; the time has come for the uncircumcised to be circumcised;... the time has come for the Kingdom of Heaven to be revealed....

'The voice of the dove is heard in our land:' What voice is this? — The voice of the King *Mashiach*."

From the interpretation by the *Midrash*, it is apparent that the root of זמירות [translated above in the verse concerning King David as "songs"] has two meanings: (a) to cut off, as in the phrase,[59] "to cut off tyrants," and (b) to sing. [These two meanings are interrelated:] Through the song of Torah study, we cut off "tyrants" — the [evil forces of] *kelipah*[60] which conceal [Divinity].

[This process is indicated by the verse,[61] "The exaltation[62] of G-d is in their throat, and a double-edged sword is in their hand."] It is *because* "the exaltation of G-d is in their throat" that "a double-edged sword is in their hand." For a double-edged sword is required to sever the nurture of the forces of evil.

---

57. [*Shir HaShirim* 2:12; see *Hemshech 5672*, Vol. I, p. 346ff.]
58. [In the course of its comment on the following verse.]
59. [Cf. *Yeshayahu* 25:5.]
60. [Literally, "shell"; hence, a metaphor in the Kabbalah for the forces of evil which obscure the G-dly core of materiality.]
61. [*Tehillim* 149:6.]
62. [I.e., the praise of G-d's loftiness. The use of this term is explained later in this *maamar*.]

To explain: The forces of evil derive their nurture in two ways: either (a) from the [transcendent spiritual light known as] *makkif;* or (b) due to the multiplicity of *tzimtzumim.*[63]

As is known, the forces of *kelipah* and the *sitra achra*[64] raise themselves aloft to receive nurture from the higher transcendent light called *makkif haelyon;* as it is written,[65] "If you make your nest high as does an eagle...," and[66] "the path of the eagle is in the heavens." [The forces of evil] can also receive nurture from the external dimensions of the transcendent light, for at this level[67] "darkness is as light," and all can receive. [I.e., since this light is unlimited, there is no distinction between good and evil recipients.]

Alternatively, [the forces of evil] can receive nurture as a result of the numerous *tzimtzumim* that exist at the end of *Hishtalshelus*, [the chainlike sequence of descending stages by which the Divine light progressively screens itself]. For the *kelipah* and the *sitra achra* cannot receive revealed light. This is implied by the teaching of our Sages[68] [in which G-d speaks of a haughty person]: "I and he cannot live [together]," [for Divine light is openly revealed only when the prospective recipient is *batel*, self-effacing].

Moreover, light can be revealed only through the medium of a receptive vessel.[69] Obviously, this does not

---

63. [I.e., stages in the self-limiting process of *tzimtzum*, by which G-d screens the extent of His revelation to make possible the existence of our material reality.]
64. [Literally, "the Other Side," i.e., forces other than those of holiness; a euphemism for the forces of evil.]
65. *[Yirmeyahu* 49:16.]
66. *[Mishlei* 30:19.]
67. *[Tehillim* 139:12.]
68. *[Sotah* 5a.]
69. [By definition, spiritual light transcends the limitations of any realm in which it radiates. If it is to be revealed and perceived, it must first be garbed in a receptor (a "vessel") which limits it and adapts it to the specific realm in which it will be revealed.]

apply to the *kelipah* and *sitra achra,* which cannot serve as vessels at all. They can receive nurture only through the numerous *tzimtzumim* [which reduce the intensity of the Divine light until] it is not revealed. In addition, [as mentioned above,] they can be nurtured by the transcendent *makkif* light — though not from its revealed aspect [for their innate self-concern prevents this], only from its external aspect.

Accordingly, to sever both conduits of the spiritual energy that nurture the forces of evil, a double-edged sword is required. This is hinted at in the verse,[70] "And I destroyed his fruit from above, and his roots from below." "I destroyed his fruit from above" — so that the forces of evil will not be able to be nurtured by the higher transcendent light; "and his roots from below" — so that they will not be able to be nurtured by the myriad *tzimtzumim.*

V

The potential for the *kelipah* and *sitra achra* to derive nurture from both these sources — from the numerous *tzimtzumim* and from *makkif haelyon,* the higher transcendent light — depends on the divine service of the Jewish people. [For indeed, all existence depends on the Jewish people.] Thus it is written, "In the beginning (בראשית), G-d created the heavens and the earth," and our Sages comment:[71] "The term ראשית ('the beginning') refers solely to the Jewish people," for whose sake the world was created. Another verse states,[72] "I made the earth, and I created (בראתי) man upon it." [Here too, the clauses of the verse suggest a dependence:] "I [i.e., He Who can truly be called 'I'] made the earth" for the sake of man. And, as our Sages

---

70. [Amos 2:9.]
71. [See *Rashi* and *Ramban* on *Bereishis* 1:1.]
72. [*Yeshayahu* 45:12.]

explain,[73] "man" refers to the Jewish people: as it is written,[74] "You are man." [The verse also alludes to] the purpose of man's creation, for בראתי ("I created") is numerically equivalent to 613: the purpose of creation is that man should observe the 613 *mitzvos* in this material world.

In this spirit our Sages teach,[75] "A person is obligated to say, 'The world was created for me,'" [i.e., for my divine service]. Since the souls of the Jewish people are the essential and ultimate reason for the creation of the world, every kind of Divine revelation and influence — even that which affects the lowest levels — depends on man, on his conduct and on his divine service.

Accordingly, through pride, haughtiness, and an overpowering sense of self-importance, [man empowers] the *kelipah* and the *sitra achra* in the heavenly worlds to raise themselves up and receive nurture from the higher transcendent light. Likewise, through lowering and demeaning himself to be drawn after a love of alien things and sinister desires, man also affects the spiritual realms: Divine light is lowered through numerous *tzimtzumim* and becomes obscured.

[This dynamic is alluded to] in the verse,[76] "Mortal man will lower himself, and the Man will be humbled." Through man's lowering himself on this material plane, i.e., following the body's undesirable tendencies to seek material desire and pleasure, the Man [i.e., the G-dly counterpart to man which is described as[77] "the image of a man"] is humbled.

---

73. [*Bava Metzia* 114b.]
74. [*Yechezkel* 34:31.]
75. [*Sanhedrin* 37a.]
76. [*Yeshayahu* 5:15, translated above to echo the mystical context of the *maamar* rather than the plain meaning of the verse.]
77. [*Yechezkel* 1:26.]

The Divine light [which maintains existence] becomes lowered through a multitude of *tzimtzumim*.

It is true that [regardless of man's conduct], through the chainlike order of spiritual descent, the measuring rod [of Divine influence] apportions [a certain measure of] nurture to the [forces of evil] through the numerous *tzimtzumim*. For they too were created [by G-d], and thus they must be granted a certain measure of vitality; as it is written,[78] "And You grant life to them all," i.e., even to the *kelipah* and *sitra achra*.

Nevertheless, they are apportioned only the precise minimum needed to maintain their existence. It is only through sins and transgressions, heaven forbid, that they are granted additional nurture, beyond what is endowed to them by the measuring rod [of Divine influence].

This concept can be understood in light of the contrast draw in *Etz Chayim, Shaar Miut HaYareach*, between the diminution [of Divine influence] brought about by the complaint of the moon,[79] and the diminution brought about by the sin of the Tree of Knowledge. In both instances, the *Sefirah* of *Malchus* was reduced to a single point, its root. Nevertheless, there is a great difference between them. In the case of the moon, [the influence of] the [preceding] nine *Sefiros* departed and ascended. With regard to the sin of the Tree of Knowledge, [the influence of] the [preceding] nine *Sefiros* was drawn down to the realm of the *kelipos*, granting them additional nurture.

---

78. [*Nechemiah* 9:6.]
79. [*Chullin* 60b (cited by *Rashi* on *Bereishis* 1:16) states that though the moon was originally created the same size as the sun, it complained: "How can two kings share a single crown?" In response, G-d answered, "Go and diminish yourself."

    The moon denotes the *Sefirah* of *Malchus*, as explained in *Etz Chayim*.]

This is a grievous matter, for sins and transgressions (heaven forbid) make the creation of *tzimtzumim* obligatory, so to speak.

By contrast, the *tzimtzumim* that exist within the chain-like process of spiritual descent are voluntary. Hence they are not genuine *tzimtzumim*, just as a limitation which is undertaken by choice is not a genuine limitation.[80] All the *tzimtzumim* through which G-d (so to speak) limited Himself [in order to bring material reality into existence] — however and wherever they were undertaken, even within the lowest realms — were not mandated by any compulsion, but were freely willed. [To paraphrase the idiom of our Sages,] thus it arose in His will.

Sins and transgressions, however, compel (so to speak) the creation of *tzimtzum*. In truth, of course, there is nothing that can compel G-d. Nevertheless, since He chose to connect Himself with the souls of the Jewish people, our conduct in this material world brings about repercussions in the spiritual realms. The *tzimtzumim* that are caused by sin are thus, as it were, imperative. This is reflected in the

---

80. [See the *maamar* entitled *Adam Ki Yakriv* (*Sefer HaMaamarim 5666*, p. 192).

A simple analogy for the presence or absence of a real limitation: If a person wants to enter a room, and his entry is blocked by a closed door or another person, he must stay outside; if, however, the door is open, the decision whether or not to enter is his alone: there is no limitation upon him.

One problem with this mortal analogy is that though the person can enter the room at will, until he actually enters he is outside. Nevertheless, this concept is used to explain how G-d is present within our material reality despite the limitations of our existence.

This difficulty can be resolved by analyzing the analogy. The room exists apart from the person; i.e., the very nature of the framework in which they both exist creates a separation between the two. With regard to G-d and the world, by contrast, nothing exists apart from Him; He is not operating within an existing framework. Therefore, when He establishes a limited framework, that limitation is only apparent, for there is no force or being requiring it. In essence, He is present within the limited framework of existence as well.]

statement of our Sages,[81] "If one walks with an upright posture..., it is as if he pushes away the stature (lit., 'the feet') of the Divine Presence." In other words, he brings about *tzimtzum*.

[By contrast,] "Positive attributes have more [powerful effects than negative ones]."[82] Every positive activity which a person performs, not only his actual observance of the Torah and its *mitzvos*, but also his positive conduct in the loving embellishment of a *mitzvah* and in his support of Torah students, gives rise to a revelation of G-dly light within the world.

This is within the capacity of each and every Jew. As it is written,[83] "For His people are G-d's portion, Yaakov is the rope of His inheritance." [The connection between G-d and His people can be compared[84] to] a rope whose upper end is tied above, and whose lower end descends below: when the lower end is shaken, the upper end also moves. Similarly, the divine service of the Jewish people in the material realm brings about corresponding influences in the spiritual realm.

VI

Every [phase in the] elevation [of a person and of materiality] comes about through divine service in prayer. For prayer (תפלה) is a process of connection, as echoed by the term,[85] "One who *joins together* (התופל) [the broken shards of] an earthenware vessel...." Prayer involves giving over one's innermost will and desire to G-d.

---

81. [*Berachos* 43b; in this context, "upright posture" implies arrogance.]
82. [*Sotah* 11a.]
83. [*Devarim* 32:9.]
84. [*Tanya, Iggeres HaTeshuvah,* ch. 6.]
85. [*Keilim* 3:5; see *Torah Or, Parshas Terumah,* p. 79d; *Sefer HaMaamarim 5709,* p. 79, and notes there.]

This is made possible through the comprehension of Divinity and through meditation, including meditation that is based on reasoning. When one meditates and grasps a divine concept until it is settled in his mind and felt in his heart, he then becomes very closely drawn to Divinity. Through the comprehension of the divine concept, he senses how lofty and precious Divinity is, and this makes it the sole focus of his entire will and desire.

There are several different levels within this approach. In certain people, this feeling — appreciating the loftiness and preciousness of Divinity — comes after the intellectual comprehension of the spiritual concept in question; i.e., when meditating on the concept, the intellectual dimension is more powerful than the resultant feeling for Divinity, which comes afterwards. After such a person grasps the idea with thorough comprehension, he then comes to a feeling for its loftiness. And as a result, the feeling he experiences is merely how "the closeness of G-d is good for [him]."[86]

At a higher level, at the time a person grasps the concept intellectually, he also feels the G-dly dimension of the subject of his meditation and comprehension, and at this same time he senses the lofty worth of Divinity. A desire for Divinity is thus aroused. This is especially true when one's divine service emanates from the inner dimension of the heart. [Though still] within the limits of intellectual reasoning, it stems from the *inner* dimension of one's mind and the attributes of the heart. In particular, this applies with regard to the revelation of *reusa delibba,* the heart's innermost spiritual desire.

---

86. [Cf. *Tehillim* 73:28. Chassidic thought explains that although this person senses the positive nature of being connected with G-dliness, his feelings are somewhat self-oriented: being close to G-d "is good for him." Ideally, one's bond with G-d should lift him entirely above feelings of self-concern.]

This is the deeper meaning of the above-quoted phrase, "the exaltation of G-d is in their throats." Meditation on the wondrous and lofty nature of the *Ein Sof,* G-d's Infinity, produces a revelation of *reusa delibba,* which redirects one's innermost will toward Divinity.

As a corresponding result in the spiritual realms, *G-d's* innermost will, i.e., the inner dimension of the transcendent *makkif* light, is drawn down in an inward manner, [i.e., in a mode of *pnimiyus,* in which it can be consciously appreciated within the world]. As a result of this, the external dimensions of the transcendent light are also drawn down in an inward manner, for the external aspects are drawn after the internal aspects. As a consequence, the *kelipah* and the *sitra achra* cannot receive nurture from the transcendent light, for it has been drawn down inwardly.

This itself also prevents the *kelipah* and the *sitra achra* from receiving nurture from the numerous *tzimtzumim.* For, as is well known, when the transcendent light shines inwardly, there is a great revelation of light throughout all the inward levels of existence, even the lowest.

Thus [G-dly meditation] severs both sources of nurture for the *kelipah* and the *sitra achra.* They can neither be nurtured by the higher transcendent light, nor by the lower levels within the G-dly light's scheme of progressive descent. This is accomplished through the divine service of prayer, [whose direction, as was stated at the beginning of this chapter, is elevation (*haalaah*).]

Torah study, by contrast, represents the drawing down (*hamshachah*) [of G-dly light] from above, so that it should be revealed. In particular, this applies with regard to the *pnimiyus* of the Torah, which refines one's intellect. Toiling in the study of the *pnimiyus* of the Torah enables one to comprehend concepts which ordinarily could not be grasped by mortal intellect.

VII

The spiritual level exemplified by [King] David was the *Sefirah* of *Malchus* (lit., "sovereignty"). His statement,[87] "I am [a man of] prayer," thus means, "I, the attribute of *Malchus,* am prayer." Nevertheless, his divine service focused on the *pnimiyus* of the Torah, through which he sought to refine [his environment].

[To explain these contrasting thrusts in divine service:] Prayer seeks to refine and elevate [worldly existence]: Torah study seeks to draw down and reveal [G-dly light]. When Torah study seeks to refine [the undesirable aspects of materiality, it does this by rejection. This is reflected in the verse,[88] "[This is the Torah...] to differentiate between the pure and the impure."

This is implied by our opening verse,[1] "Your statutes were my songs when I dwelled in fear." With the power of the Torah, [David] would cut off [the forces of evil which are known as] "tyrants"; [i.e., he refined his environment] in the spirit of [the statement of our Sages,][89] "He glanced at him, and he became a pile of bones."

This, however, [is not G-d's intent in creation]: the world was not created for chaos, but in order that it be settled.[90] [This requires that man] involve himself with the tasks of refining [his environment] and drawing down G-dly light into the world. For this reason [David] was punished, [for ignoring this thrust and seeking to rise above worldly existence].

On this basis, [we can reconcile the queries raised at the outset regarding the verse,] "G-d is among those who help me." A person's true helpers are the elements [of worldly

---

87. *[Tehillim 109:4, and see Ibn Ezra and Metzudas David.]*
88. *[Vayikra 11:[46-]47.]*
89. *[Berachos 58a; Shabbos 34a.]*
90. [Cf. *Yeshayahu* 45:18.]

existence] which he has refined. Just as our Sages[91] refer to one's students as one's "children", the G-dly sparks [which a person] has refined [can be termed his "helpers"].

[Included in the Hebrew original of the verse, "G-d is among those who help me," is the phrase, הוי-ה לי — lit., "G-d is *for me*." Hence:] When a person devotes himself in an orderly manner to his Divinely-appointed task of refinement, a revelation of *Havayah* shines forth *upon him*. Moreover, "G-d is *among* [lit., *within*] those who help me": Through a person's self-sacrifice in carrying out his divine service, he brings about a revelation of *Havayah* within all those who help him.

[As an automatic result of this revelation,] "I [will] witness [the downfall of] those who hate me." Just as in the verse,[92] "He swallowed wealth but will vomit it up," through his divine service man is able to extract the G-dly sparks [hidden in materiality], and then its evil trappings are automatically nullified.

[By way of a parallel, one may cite the mystical interpretation of the directive of the *Haggadah* concerning the רשע, the wicked son]: הקהה את שיניו — "Blunt his teeth." [The last Hebrew word can also be understood to mean "his [letter] *shin*." Hence, "blunting the wicked son's teeth" involves] removing the ש from the word רשע, leaving the word רע, meaning "evil". [Since, as discussed in the Kabbalah, the letter *shin* conveys G-dly influence,[93] the wicked son's existence depends on it. When it is removed, the evil will automatically be nullified,] for evil cannot exist independently. [Similarly, through our labors in refining our physical environment, we liberate the G-dly sparks embed-

---

91. [Prologue to *Esther Rabbah*, sec. 11, quoted above in the *maamar* entitled *VeKibeil HaYehudim*, sec. 1.]
92. [*Iyov* 20:15.]
93. [*Zohar* I, 2b; see also *Basi LeGani*, ch. 6.]

ded there, and then the purely material (i.e., the evil) dimensions of existence are nullified.]

On this basis, we can also resolve our opening questions regarding the statement of our Sages,[16] "A person who comes to purify [himself] is granted assistance." The plural form is used [for the verb "granted assistance"], to refer to the many G-dly sparks which he refines.

This also explains why the transitive form [of the infinitive לטהר] is used — for as a result of one's own self-refinement and the revelation of G-dly light in the world, one purifies others as well. In particular, this applies with regard to teaching Torah publicly, for[94] "the Torah is light," and this generates merit for the public.

This is the meaning of David's request, "May I witness [the downfall of] those who hate me." Although they included individuals such as Doeg and Achitofel who appeared to conduct their lives according to the Torah, David made this request with the intent that the truth be revealed — that these individuals hated G-d: they did not desire the revelation of G-dliness, and [more particularly,] the revelation of the Name *Havayah*, [which transcends the limits of nature]. They desired to live by the natural order and mortal reason. This is the direct opposite of the true unity expressed in the above-quoted statement,[5] "*Havayah* and *Elokim* are all one."

We can now appreciate the juxtaposition of the two clauses of the verse: When "G-d is among those who help me," *then* "I [will] witness [the downfall of] those who hate me." The level of *sight* [is the level hinted at in the teaching,[95]] "Who is a wise man? — One who *sees the future*" [lit., "who sees that which is to be born," a phrase which

---

94. [*Mishlei* 6:23.]
95. [*Tamid* 32a.]

allows for an extended meaning:[96] "who sees how every entity comes into existence from absolute nothingness"]. Perceiving G-d's sublime unity at this level is known as *Yichuda Ilaah*. And it is solely through [confronting] opposition [that this level can be attained].

When this takes place, "G-d [will be] among my helpers": All those who help a person will also be granted a revelation of the Name *Havayah*. Thus, too, it is written,[97] "If you extract the precious from the vulgar, you shall be as My mouth." [I.e., when a person succeeds in refining his environment by bringing out the precious G-dliness that is hidden in a vulgar setting, he comes to resemble G-d's "mouth", a vehicle for the expression of G-dliness].

As a result, the G-dliness which transcends nature will be revealed within the natural order, as in the phrase,[98] "to see the *face* of G-d." [פנים, the Hebrew for "face", suggests פנימיות, meaning "the inner dimension."] The inner dimension of *Elokim*, [the Name of G-d which is manifest within the natural order,] is *Havayah*, the attribute of openly revealed compassion and kindness.

And every kindness which G-d grants a person should motivate him to be extremely humble,[99] and to seek abundant mercy for his soul, [requesting] that G-d grant him assistance to toil in the study of Torah and in the service of G-d, so as to fulfill His intent [in creation] — for "the Holy One, blessed be He, desired a dwelling in the lower realms."[100]

---

96. [*Tanya*, beginning of ch. 43.]
97. [Cf. *Yirmeyahu* 15:19.]
98. [Cf. *Tehillim* 42:3.]
99. [See *Tanya* — *Iggeres HaKodesh*, Epistle 2.]
100. [*Midrash Tanchuma, Parshas Bechukosai*, sec. 3; see *Tanya*, chs. 33 and 36.]

Maamar
Baruch HaGomel
LaChayavim Tovos
5687 [1927]

מאמר
ברוך הגומל
לחייבים טובות
תרפ"ז

"BLESSED [ARE YOU...] WHO BESTOWS
GOOD THINGS UPON THE CULPABLE..."

[This *maamar*, which opens and closes with the theme of thanksgiving, was delivered on Wednesday, the thirteenth of Tammuz, just before the Rebbe Rayatz was released – after ten days – from Kostroma, the city to which he had been exiled for three years.]

I

[A person saved from a life-threatening situation expresses his thanksgiving in the following words:][1] ברוך... הגומל לחייבים טובות שגמלני טוב — "Blessed [are You...] Who bestows good things upon the culpable,[2] Who has bestowed goodness upon me." Now, why does the wording of this blessing differ from that of the blessing recited when a miracle occurs:[3] ברוך [אתה...] שעשה לי נס... — "Blessed [are You...] Who performed a miracle for me..."? To match this, our blessing should surely have been worded, ברוך [אתה...] שעשה לי טוב — "Blessed [are You...] Who performed something good for me."

[We can resolve this question by first clarifying a related concept.] As is well known, the descent of the soul into the body, however awesome, is a descent for the purpose of ascent.[4] The [Divine] soul descends to this lowly plane, to be garbed within a body and an *animal* soul. This descent is particularly formidable in the time of exile, when numerous obstacles and hindrances hamper the study of the Torah and the observance of the *mitzvos*, as well as the bothersome worries and stresses of earning a livelihood.

---

1. [*Rambam, Hilchos Berachos* 10:8; *Siddur Tehillat HaShem*, p. 186].
2. [I.e., the unworthy.]
3. [*Berachos* 54a; *Seder Birkas HaNehenin* 13:1].
4. [In the original, *yeridah tzorech aliyah*; cf. *Tanya*, ch. 31.]

Suppose, however, that a Jew overcomes his nature. With powerful determination, he sets aside time to engage in the study of the Torah and in "the service of the heart, i.e., prayer,"[5] and to observe the *mitzvos* with pure faith and with an unquestioning acceptance of the yoke of heaven. Undaunted by any obstacle or hindrance, he stands firm in his conviction to study and to teach. In such a case, it is specifically this kind of divine service that elevates the soul to a higher level than its position before it descended into the body.

[The source for this determination is alluded to in the chassidic interpretation of] our Sages' statement:[6] משביעים אותו, תהי צדיק ואל תהי רשע — "[In heaven, before a Jew is born,] an oath is administered to him: 'Be righteous, and do not be wicked.'" The term *tzaddik* implies innocence and the term *rasha* implies guilt. As is well known,[7] administering this oath to the soul can also be understood as investing it ("sating" it) with power. [The root (שבע) of the verb משביעים ("an oath is administered") is virtually identical with the root (שבע) of the verb משביעים ("one causes [him] to be sated").] When the soul is about to descend to this physical plane to be enclothed within the body, it is invested with the requisite power to overcome the material orientation of the body and conquer the animal soul, and to contend with all the veils and obscurities that screen the light of the soul.[8]

---

5. [See *Sifri, Devarim* 11:3; *Taanis* 2a.]
6. [*Niddah* 30b].
7. [*Kitzurim VeHearos LeTanya* by the *Tzemach Tzedek*, pp. 48ff., 165ff.; *Sefer HaMaamarim 5698*, p. 235ff. In English, see *Lessons In Tanya*, Vol. I, p. 31].
8. [It is the proper use of this power that elevates the soul beyond its original level.]

II

By way of explanation: Our Sages (*Kiddushin* 30b) teach that "every day a person's [Evil] Inclination rises powerfully against him and desires to slay him, as it is written,[9] 'The wicked watches out for the righteous, and seeks to slay him.' Were it not for the Holy One, blessed be He, Who helps him, a man would not be able [to contend] with it, as it is written,[10] 'G-d does not abandon him to his hand.'"

There is a verse [alluding to the *kelipah*] that says,[11] "The leech has two daughters [who cry], 'Give, give!'" In this spirit, the Evil Inclination naturally has a greedy disposition[12] which desires and craves whatever physical and material benefits it sees. Its spirit is haughty, [causing a person] to be precious in his own eyes, to exalt himself over others, and to pursue honor and glorification. He does not begrudge others what they own. Not only does he consider his own possessions as being intended for himself alone, but in addition he is envious and craves the possessions of others. All day and all night he pursues the desires and fancies of his heart like an animal. His intellectual activity is directed only toward fulfilling his desires and contriving to satisfy the cravings of his heart.

III

To explain: Our Sages declare,[13] "The Evil Inclination is like a fly sitting between the two openings of the heart." Its only concern is its own desires and yearnings. Like a mosquito which takes nurture into its body, but does not give forth, so too, the animal soul thinks only of itself. As it is

---

9. [*Tehillim* 37:32].
10. [*Ibid.*, v. 33].
11. [*Mishlei* 30:15; *Tanya*, ch. 19; *Likkutei Torah, Parshas Masei*, 91b].
12. [Cf. *Avos* 5:19.]
13. [*Berachos* 61a].

said,[14] "The eye sees and the heart craves." Likewise, the *Jerusalem Talmud (Berachos* 1:5) states: "The eyes and the heart are two brokers for sin." [The process] begins with sight. As our Sages comment *(Sotah* 8a), "The Evil Inclination does not rule over anything unless it can see it." After a person sees something, his heart begins to hanker after it, and he follows its whims.

The basic reason for this is a person's exceeding self-love, his high regard for himself. This is why he indulges himself, allowing his heart free rein without any restraint or limit. Not only does he not fear G-d at all,[15] but he acts like a wild animal, attacking and stealing in many different ways to fulfill his heart's desires.

As we see for ourselves, there are people who follow the desires of their hearts, heaven forbid; all their thoughts, words and deeds are oriented to what they crave. This attitude results from the seductive craft of the Evil Inclination which incites a person, and leads him from one downfall to the next, heaven forbid.

IV

The appropriate response is indicated by our Sages *(Kiddushin* 30b): "I [G-d] created the Evil Inclination, and I created the Torah as a condiment [to temper] it. If you are occupied in the study of the Torah, you will not be delivered into his hand.... If you are confronted by that despicable one ('i.e., if the Evil Inclination aggravates you' — *Rashi*), drag him to the House of Study. If he is like a stone, he will crumble; if he is like iron, he will be crushed." The Evil Inclination has several different [forms of expression]. There are people whose hearts are like stone, heaven forbid, and others whose hearts are like iron.

---

14. [*Rashi* on *Bamidbar* 15:39, paraphrasing *Bamidbar Rabbah* 10:2].
15. [Cf. *Tehillim* 36:2.]

In either case, the Evil Inclination makes these people resemble inanimate objects. Just as an object cannot be responsive to a concept, for the two are qualitatively worlds apart, so too, such a person is not at a level at which he can be affected by a Divine concept. Like a stone, he feels no vitality in his study of the Torah or in the observance of its *mitzvos*.

This situation can be rectified through the study of Torah and attendance at the House of Study. This is implied by our Sages' statement, "If you are occupied in the study of the Torah...." This means not only studying oneself (or listening to communal study sessions if one is incapable of studying alone), but working to disseminate Torah study among others. We find this implied in the verse,[16] "Out of the mouths of babes and sucklings You established strength." And our Sages comment,[17] "'Strength' really refers to the Torah." Such a person, then, attends the House of Study to join in communal prayer; he participates in fixed study sessions before and after [morning] prayers, as well as between the afternoon and evening services, and whenever communal study is conducted wherever he may be.

Through such activities, the Evil Inclination crumbles. As may plainly be observed, individuals who have engaged in the study of the Torah in different ways have thereby risen to a high spiritual level. When even a simple person, who is unable to study alone, dedicates himself to supporting Torah scholars, he elevates the standing of his soul, and becomes included in the category of "masters of good deeds."[18] In [many] other sources,[19] the great merit of those involved in such activities is extolled. For example (*Berachos* 5a): "Suffering will stay far from those who

---

16. [*Tehillim* 8:3. See the above *maamar* entitled *VeKibeil HaYehudim 5687.*]
17. [*Midrash Tehillim* on the above-quoted verse; *Shir HaShirim Rabbah* 1:4].
18. [*Tanya* — *Iggeres HaKodesh*, the latter part of Epistle 5; *Biurei HaZohar* of the Mitteler Rebbe, p. 25a-b].
19. [See *Sefer HaMaamarim 5698*, p. 35.]

occupy themselves in Torah study," and it is stated (in *Avodah Zarah* 19b) that the possessions of such people will prosper.[20]

V

At the time of the Giving of the Torah, all the Jewish people whose souls were then enclothed in bodies, as well as the souls of all the Jewish people which will be enclothed in bodies until the coming of *Mashiach*[21] (*May this be speedily in our days!*), all undertook the observance of the Torah and its *mitzvos,* as one man[22] — on behalf of ourselves, our children, and our grandchildren.

[Towards the end of the saga of the Purim miracle,] it is written:[23] קימו וקבלו היהודים — "The Jews affirmed and accepted...." The Sages [connect this with an earlier episode]:[24] קימו מה שקבלו כבר — "They now affirmed [i.e., integrated within themselves] what they had already accepted [when the Torah was given]." In the present time of exile, when obstacles and hindrances to the study of the Torah and the observance of its *mitzvos* multiply, — this is the time to intensify our divine service in their fulfillment.

[Throughout history, challenges to our people's faith have stirred them to the peaks of divine service.] For example, in the era of Mordechai and Esther, Haman sought to raise his hand[25] against the Jews, his sole ambition being to destroy our people[26] and uproot their faith. Similarly, [at the time of the Hasmonean uprising commemorated by

---

20. [See also *Sefer HaMaamarim 5687,* pp. 103, 107; *Sefer HaMaamarim — Kuntreisim,* Vol. I, p. 515 ff.]
21. [See *Pirkei deRabbi Eliezer,* ch. 41; *Shmos Rabbah,* end of sec. 28.]
22. [*Mechilta* and *Rashi* on *Shmos* 19:2].
23. [*Esther* 9:27].
24. [*Shabbos* 88a].
25. [Cf. *Esther* 3:6.]
26. [Cf. *ibid.,* 8:5.]

Chanukah], the Greeks sought to provoke [our people into a denial of G-d and His Torah, demanding],[27] "Inscribe it on the horn of an ox [i.e., indelibly] that you have no share in the G-d of Israel." It was precisely these times that emboldened our people to summon the strength needed to observe the Torah and its *mitzvos* with *mesirus nefesh,* in a spirit of self-sacrifice, as is explained elsewhere.

It is written,[28] "I, G-d, have not changed, nor have you, Jacob's descendants, expired (לא כליתם)." [Beyond its simple meaning, the verse may also be understood at the non-literal level of *derush.*] The prophet exclaims in wonderment: You, the Jewish people, see that G-d has not retracted His commitment [to you], as it is written,[29] כי לא יטוש ה' עמו ונחלתו לא יעזוב — "For G-d will not abandon His people, nor will He forsake His inheritance." Everyone can see Divine Providence palpably, for our people are[30] "one lamb among seventy wolves, and yet it survives." If so, [the prophet asks the Jewish people,] why are you not drawn after the Torah and its *mitzvos* [with a love so intense that] your soul expires (כלות הנפש)?

For witnessing overt Divine Providence should surely motivate a person to dedicate himself to the Torah and its *mitzvos.* If, for whatever reason, his involvement does not reflect his true ability and potential, he is aroused from above, and is saved.

This, then, is the inner message of [the conclusion of the Blessing of Thanksgiving, which blesses Him] "Who has bestowed goodness (טוב) upon me." [Using the same Hebrew noun,] our Sages teach,[31] אין טוב אלא תורה — "There

---

27. [*Yerushalmi, Chagigah* 2:2; *Megillas Taanis,* ch. 2; *Bereishis Rabbah* 2:4, 16:7; *Torah Or, Parshas Vayeishev,* p. 30a].
28. [*Malachi* 3:6].
29. [*Tehillim* 94:14].
30. [*Tanchuma, Parshas Toldos,* sec. 5; *Esther Rabbah* 10:11].
31. [*Avos* 6:3].

is no [true] good other than the Torah." [Hence, in reciting this blessing, the individual expresses thanks for the opportunity] to apply himself with increased vigor to serving G-d through Torah study and prayer.[32]

---

32. [In a sequel to this *maamar*, also entitled *Baruch HaGomel*, delivered a few days later on the *Shabbos (Parshas Pinchas)* following *Yud-Gimmel* Tammuz, the Rebbe Rayatz answered the question with which our *maamar* opened: Since the obligations of the Torah and its *mitzvos* are eternal, whereas all of exile's obstacles are merely challenges, a person who (for whatever reason) does not fulfill his obligations *acknowledges his culpability* — and also thanks Him "Who bestows good things [even] upon the culpable."]

Maamar	מאמר
Asarah SheYoshvim	עשרה שיושבים
VeOskim BaTorah	ועוסקים בתורה
5688 [1928]	תרפ״ח

"WHEN TEN PEOPLE SIT AND OCCUPY THEMSELVES WITH TORAH STUDY…"

[Soon after his release from imprisonment and exile, the Rebbe Rayatz moved to Riga, Latvia. A year later, though contact with his chassidim in Russia was problematic, he sent them the following letter, dated 15 Sivan, the anniversary of his arrest, together with the *maamar* which is reproduced below. On several occasions the Rebbe had these two documents reprinted and he often suggested that they be studied as part of the celebration of *Yud-Beis-Yud-Gimmel Tammuz.*]

THE LETTER SENT BY THE PREVIOUS REBBE FOR THE FIRST ANNIVERSARY CELEBRATION OF YUD-BEIS TAMMUZ IN 5688 (1928)

By the Grace of G-d,
Sunday, 15 Sivan, 5688, Riga.

To our friends, the members of the chassidic brotherhood, and to all those who love the Torah and study it — wherever you may be: May G-d be with you.

Greetings and blessings:

Today marks the first day of my incarceration in the Spalerno Prison in Leningrad, in Section Six, Cell 160, during the night preceding the Wednesday of the week in which one reads the verse [in *Parshas Shlach*[1]], "And now, let the strength of G-d be magnified" — on the fifteenth of the month of Sivan, 5687 [1927]. There I was maltreated until the Sunday preceding the *Shabbos* on which one reads the verse [in *Parshas Balak*[2]], "How goodly are your tents, O

---

1. [*Bamidbar* 14:17.]
2. [*Ibid.* 24:5.]

Yaakov, and your dwelling-places, O Yisrael" — the third of the month of Tammuz. On that day I was forced to leave for a three-year exile in Kostrama.

It is clear to everyone that the imprisonment and exile were brought upon me by the calumnies of our brethren who hate us and despise us, by men who — in defiance of the laws of the land and its government — persecute those who observe the laws of Moshe and Israel.

These people could not bear to see how the rose of Yaakov flourished, as the study of the Torah was disseminated throughout the length and breadth of this land. They therefore trumped up false libels in order to bring about my downfall, and thereby (G-d forbid) to destroy the House of Yaakov.

But G-d's acts of kindness are never-ending, and the merit of our holy forefathers has not been exhausted — and will never be exhausted — in protection of those who walk in their paths. Thus it was that freedom was granted to me on the twelfth day of Tammuz, on the Tuesday preceding the *Shabbos* on which one reads the verse [in *Parshas Pinchas*[3]], "I hereby grant him My covenant of peace."

It was not myself alone that the Holy One, blessed be He, redeemed on *Yud-Beis* Tammuz, but also those who love the Torah and observe its commands, and so too all those who merely bear the name "Jew"[4] — for the heart of every man of Israel (irrespective of his particular level in the observance of the *mitzvos*) is perfectly bound with G-d and His Torah.

---

3. [Ibid. 25:12.]
4. As the Rebbe points out, the term "bear the name" (יכונה) has a distinct technical meaning in Jewish law: a כינוי is a name other than one's given name, which is perhaps not widely used. Here this usage alludes to people estranged from their Jewish identities to the point that "Jew" is a name used by others and not by themselves. It is nevertheless appropriate, as is made clear by the continuation of the above sentence of the *maamar*.

Today, the twelfth of the month of Tammuz, is the Festival of Liberation of all Jews who are involved in the dissemination of Torah knowledge, for on this day it became known and manifest to everyone that the great work in which I labored in the dissemination of the Torah and in the strengthening of the religion *is permitted according to the law of the land,* which grants freedom of worship to those who observe the [Jewish] religion as it does to all the citizens of this country.

This is the day on which the light of the merit of public Torah study banished the misty gloom of calumnies and libels. It is fitting that such a day be set aside as a day of *farbrengen* — a day on which people arouse each other to fortify Torah study and the practice of *Yiddishkeit* in every place according to its needs, a day on which to offer blessings to our brethren in Russia (who are suffering from such libelers and informers), that G-d strengthen their hearts and the hearts of their children so that they will remain faithful Jews, and never again be persecuted by the above-mentioned evildoers.

With the auspicious approach of the Festival of Liberation of all those who engage in the dissemination of Torah, I hereby offer my blessings to all our brethren who love the Torah and study it, and to all those who publicly teach the Torah: May G-d open up His goodly storehouse and grant them, together with all of our brethren of the House of Israel, abounding life and endless blessing; may He fortify their hearts so that they will courageously extend their dissemination of Torah knowledge and their buttressing of *Yiddishkeit;* and may we all be spared to see children and grandchildren engaging in Torah and *mitzvos,* free of care or want.

* * *

At the beginning of the year 5687 (תרפ״ז; 1926) I made a request to the chassidic brotherhood — that every group of worshipers in the synagogues after *Shacharis* should make a regular practice of reading the daily allotment of *Tehillim* as apportioned throughout each month, and that this be followed by *Kaddish,* according to custom.⁵ This request *still*

---

5. [The Rebbe appended the following note to the above letter by the Rebbe Rayatz:] "In order to clarify the chronology of events, we hereby reproduce a passage from the account of *The Imprisonment and the Liberation* of the Rebbe, my revered father-in-law, in 5687 (תרפ״ז; 1927), written by a friend of the Rebbe's household — the esteemed and venerable chassid, R. Eliyahu Chayim ben R. Pinchas Todros Althaus *(May G-d avenge his martyrdom!)."*

The passage reads as follows: "From the beginning of that fateful year, 5687, a fearful dread overcame all those who felt close to the Rebbe, the House of our Life. The fear reached even the Rebbe himself, as my friend R. Michael Dvorkin and I heard explicitly from his holy mouth in Kostrama, the town to which the Rebbe was exiled [after his reprieve on *Yud-Gimmel Tammuz*]. These were his very words, letter by letter: 'Before 5687 I was very much afraid. It was not myself I was anxious about; I was thinking about the chassidim. I experienced great difficulty in finally issuing the directive that people should start reciting *Tehillim.'*

"'When was the directive issued?' I asked.

"'On Simchas Torah,' replied the Rebbe.

"I then recalled that on Simchas Torah that year, at the *Kiddush* that was held in the room of his mother, the *Rebbitzin* [Sterna Sarah], the Rebbe had repeatedly asked the members of the chassidic brotherhood to undertake *(bli neder)* to read the daily allotment of *Tehillim* according to the monthly cycle — in all the *minyanim* after *Shacharis,* with *Kaddish* following. I recall that I asked him if I would discharge my obligation by the *Tehillim* that I read every day before *davenen.*

"The Rebbe replied in these words: 'The *Tehillim* that one reads before [the morning's] *davenen* is connected to *Tikkun Chatzos.'*

"All in all, the talks of the Rebbe on that Simchas Torah were pervaded by a spirit of bitterness, coming from a contrite and shattered heart.

"I have no doubt that the well-known penciled note concerning the reading of *Tehillim* that we found in the Rebbe's study on the dread day of his imprisonment had also been written in Elul 5686 or in Tishrei 5687. This is my conclusion, because though it was undated, it concludes with his blessing for 'a happy year,' as people are accustomed to do either at the end of a year or at the beginning of the next.

"This is a copy of the note that was found on a high table in the Rebbe's study after he had been imprisoned on Wednesday, 15 Sivan 5687, in Len-

stands — for the public good. (Indeed, it would be proper to institute this practice in every *shul,* for it is not relevant to chassidim alone.⁶) And by virtue of this reading, may all those concerned be blessed by the Source of Blessings with all manner of bounty both spiritual and material.

* * *

For all the members of our chassidic brotherhood I am enclosing the *maamar* which begins, *Asarah SheYoshvim VeOskim BaTorah, Shechinah Sheruyah Beineihem.* May our

---

ingrad: 'Chassidim, and all Jews who are waiting in hope for *Mashiach:* listen! Pass the word on in my name to all chassidim around the world — that I have directed that in all chassidic *shuls,* after *Shacharis* every day (including *Shabbos*), *Tehillim* should be read communally by the congregation according to the monthly cycle, and this reading should be followed by *Kaddish.* Moreover, all the businessmen and market folk who cherish the homely warmth of yore should go to *shul* to pray, and should be present [between *Minchah* and *Maariv*] during the communal study of *Ein Yaakov.* And the A-lmighty will enable them to earn a comfortable livelihood.

"'When you speak to chassidim, tell them this comes from me as a directive; when you speak to other Jews, tell them that out of the love of a fellow Jew, and out of concern for the welfare of a fellow Jew, I ask them to fulfill the above requests.

"'May the A-lmighty bless us all with a happy year, both spiritually and materially, and may we be privileged to experience a complete Redemption through *Mashiach, Amen.*" (*Kovetz Michtavim,* the letters appended to *Tehillim Ohel Yosef Yitzchak,* Kehot, N.Y., p. 210.)

6. In the course of the years that have elapsed since the above was written, many congregations, both those who pray according to *Nussach Ari* as well as others, have instituted the practice of reciting, after *Shacharis* every day and after *Musaf* on *Shabbos* and festivals, a section of the Book of *Tehillim* as it is apportioned according to the days of the month. After *Tehillim,* the Mourner's *Kaddish* is said. Every *Shabbos Mevarchim* (the *Shabbos* before Rosh Chodesh), including the *Shabbos* preceding Rosh HaShanah, early in the morning before *Shacharis,* the entire Book of *Tehillim* is recited, followed by the Mourner's *Kaddish.* If a congregant observing *yahrzeit* or a mourner is present, the Mourner's *Kaddish* is said after each of the five Books of *Tehillim.*

A further custom, first introduced on Sunday, the second of Nissan, 5704: On those days when *Tachanun* is not said, and therefore Psalm 20 (למנצח וגו' יענך) is not said [at *Shacharis*], this Psalm is read after *Shacharis* — not as part of it, but as the opening passage of *Tehillim.*

eyes witness the ascending glory of the Torah, of Israel, and of our brotherhood, and may we behold the goodly light.

Your unswerving friend, who seeks the welfare and success of yourselves and your children and grandchildren, and who blesses you all both materially and spiritually,

(—)

Asarah SheYoshvim VeOskim BaTorah

I

When[1] ten people sit and occupy themselves with Torah study, the Divine Presence rests among them, as it is said,[2] "G-d stands in the assembly of the L-rd." [The word "assembly" indicates a minimum of ten *(Rashi)*.] From where do we learn that the same is true even of five? For it is said:[3] "He has founded His band on the earth." [The word "band" refers to a group of five *(Rashi, Rambam, Rabbeinu Yonah)*.] From where do we learn that the same is true even of three? For it is said:[4] "Amidst the judges, He renders judgment." [A court comprises three judges *(Rashi)*.] From where do we learn that the same is true even of two? For it is said:[5] "Then the G-d-fearing conversed with each other and G-d hearkened and heard." And from where do we learn that the same is true even of one? For it is said:[6] "In every place where I will have My Name mentioned [i.e., that I will inspire your heart with the wisdom to mention My name *(Rashi)*], I will come [there] to you [the singular form is used] and bless you."

Thus, even one individual who sits and occupies himself with Torah, draws down G-dliness. Nevertheless, there is a difference between the Torah study of a single individual

---

1. [Avos 3:6. In the original, the passage begins as follows: עשרה שיושבים ועוסקים בתורה, שכינה שרוי-ה ביניהם.]
2. [Tehillim 82:1.]
3. [Amos 9:6.]
4. [Tehillim, loc. cit.]
5. [Malachi 3:16.]
6. [Shmos 20:21.]

and that of a group.⁷ A group draws down a higher level [of Divine light].

We see a parallel in the realm of prayer. Our Sages teach:⁸ "The prayer of the community will never be despised, as is implied by the verse:⁹ 'The mighty G-d will not despise.'" This is because, through their prayers, the community draw down the Thirteen Attributes of Mercy. Similarly, the Torah study of the community draws down the revelation of a higher light than does the study of an individual.

[The correlation between prayer and study is emphasized by the interrelation of the Thirteen Attributes of Mercy which are elicited by communal prayer, and] the thirteen principles of Biblical interpretation enumerated by Rabbi Yishmael: *kal vachomer, gezeirah shavah,* and so on.¹⁰

These thirteen principles are mediums for the revelation of the light of Torah; i.e., each of these thirteen principles reflects a new approach to study. For example, the first of these principles, the *kal vachomer* [a conclusion drawn from a minor premise to a major one], reveals a new concept in the Torah. Similarly, all these principles are sources of Torah, revealing new dimensions of Torah; i.e., each principle reveals the light of Torah openly and in a more specific manner.

This is because these thirteen principles of Biblical exegesis correspond to the Thirteen Attributes of Mercy.¹¹ This

---

7. See also *Berachos* 6a, and the commentaries on the above-quoted *mishnah* from *Avos.*
8. [*Berachos* 8a.]
9. [*Iyov* 36:5.]
10. [*Sifra,* Introduction. In the above text, the phrase introducing the list ends with the word נדרשת.] The commentary of *Rashbam* (on *Bava Basra* 111a, s.v. מדין), and likewise the author of *Kerisos* adds the word בהן, but this is not our version of the text [See *Siddur Tehillat HaShem,* p. 25.].
11. See conclusion of the second *maamar* entitled *Ani LeDodi* in *Likkutei Torah, Parshas Re'eh.*

was emphasized by the Maggid of Mezritch in his interpretation [of the prayers of Moshe Rabbeinu on behalf of his stricken sister, Miriam]. When Moshe Rabbeinu evoked the first of the Thirteen Attributes of Mercy, the Divine Name א-ל, praying,[12] "Please G-d, heal her," G-d responded with a *kal vachomer*. As the verse relates:[13] "And G-d said to Moshe: ['Had her father spat in her face,] would she not be embarrassed for seven days?...'" For, as our Sages (*Bava Kama* 25a) comment, [the conclusion drawn from shame inflicted by a father, to shame caused by G-d] is a *kal vachomer*.

Thus, just as the Thirteen Attributes of Mercy draw down the thirteen principles of exegesis — as in the example quoted above, the attribute א-ל drew down the principle of *kal vachomer* — conversely, through the thirteen principles of Biblical exegesis as a whole, we draw down the revelation of the Thirteen Attributes of Mercy.

[This interrelation is also emphasized by two different interpretations] of the phrase,[14] "the shepherd among the roses." [Noting that the Hebrew for "roses," שושנים, shares the same letters as ששונים, "those who study,"] our Sages comment:[15] "Do not read 'among the roses,' read '[among] those who study [Torah law].'"

The *Zohar* (Introduction), [however, interprets the same phrase as a reference to the Thirteen Attributes of Mercy]: "What does the rose represent? — The congregation of Israel. Just as a rose has thirteen petals, so, too, the congregation of Israel has Thirteen Attributes of Mercy which surround it on all sides."

---

12. [*Bamidbar* 12:13.]
13. [*Loc. cit.*, v. 14.]
14. [*Shir HaShirim* 6:3.]
15. [Cf. *Shabbos* 30b.]

Thus, [this also points out that] the Thirteen Attributes of Mercy are drawn down to this world through the study of Torah.

II

Students of Torah in general, and in particular, teachers of Torah, are referred to as[16] "guardians of the city," [indicating that the protective influence which stems] from the Thirteen Attributes of Mercy drawn down by Torah study is essentially dependent on public Torah study. This concept can also be explained through a comparison to prayer. Prayer is a process of elevation initiated from below; i.e., an arousal from below which awakens an arousal from above, the nature of the arousal from above [being determined by and therefore] *corresponding* to the arousal from below. Communal prayer, [however, defies this principle]. Through its prayer, the community draws down a higher level of arousal from above, which is of a different nature than the elevation of מ"נ (divine service initiated from below[17]) which they generated. Communal prayer is thus superior in that the arousal from above does not correspond to the arousal generated from below.

[The arousal from above always surpasses the arousal from below. In regard to the prayer of an individual, however, there is a direct and proportionate correspondence between the two. In regard to communal prayer, by contrast, the arousal from above utterly surpasses the arousal from below.]

On this basis, we can understand our Sages' interpretation of the verse quoted above: "The mighty G-d will not

---

16. *Yerushalmi, Chagigah* 1:7; beginning of *Eichah Rabbah*.
17. [In the Kabbalistic metaphor describing the dynamic of love between G-d and His people, the "elevation of *mayin nukvin*" (whose acronym is מ"נ) signifies an initiative taken by the "feminine" (or recipient) element; hence, a step in divine service initiated by the Jewish people.]

despise." [How is it possible to promise that G-d will never despise a prayer?] Indeed, were the arousal from above to be dependent on the arousal from below, it would be impossible to make such a promise. It is possible that the elevation of מ"ץ would evoke such a response. Since, as explained above, in regard to communal prayer, the arousal from above does not correspond to the arousal from below because communal prayer is superior to individual prayer, [it is possible to promise that G-d will not despise it.]

[We find a parallel concept to this] regarding private prayers during the Ten Days of Repentance. As our Sages state:[18] "When is it possible for an individual [to attain superior heights of Divine perception]? — During the ten days from Rosh HaShanah to Yom Kippur," when he draws down the Thirteen Attributes of Mercy, as is generally accomplished through communal prayer. At this time, [the influence he arouses] does not correspond to the nature of his service. Therefore, this occurs [only] during the Ten Days of Repentance, which is "a time of Divine gratification." Similarly, throughout the year, communal prayer draws down the Thirteen Attributes of Mercy, bringing about a response from above which outshines man's devout initiatives.

Similar concepts apply regarding Torah study. In general, Torah study involves a drawing down of Divine influence from above. Nevertheless, this can only come about through an arousal from below. The Torah is a revelation *from above* only insofar as the influence drawn down does not correspond to the arousal from below. "Revelation from above" is thus not an adequate description, for Torah study requires work and exertion.

[This toil and exertion does not refer to one's efforts in study alone, but also to one's struggle for personal refine-

---

18. [*Yevamos* 49b.]

ment.] This is alluded to in our Sages' statement:[19] "Whoever claims, 'There is nothing for me other than Torah,' does not even possess Torah." Rather, [together with Torah study,] one must also serve G-d through prayer.[20]

Apart from the labor and effort that are necessary for Torah study in its own right — as implied by our Sages' statement,[21] "You labored and you found," for the development of an intellectual concept requires work — one thereby changes one's habits. This is implied by the teaching of our Sages,[22] "There is no comparison between one who reviews his studies one hundred times and one who does so one hundred and one times." [Indeed, the additional review, beyond one's usual habit, entitles him] to be called "one who serves G-d."

The very first stage of service is to change one's habits.[23] For this reason, G-d's first statement to Avraham was:[24] "Go

---

19. *Ibid.* 109b.
20. "[The context of the above teaching underscores the intention of our Sages] — that one must combine Torah study with kindly deeds. These 'deeds' (*gemilus chassadim*) must surely be understood simply and literally, for 'the ultimate end of wisdom is *teshuvah* and good deeds' (*Berachos* 17a); moreover: 'It would have been preferable for a person who studies Torah, but does not apply it, never to have been born' (cf. *Tanchuma* on *Parshas Eikev,* sec. 6). Nevertheless, concentration during prayer is also considered an 'act of kindness' (cf. *Rashi* on *Shabbos* 127b)." (See end of sec. 3 of the explanation in *Likkutei Torah* of the *maamar* beginning *Velo Tashbis.*)

    Significantly, the conclusion of the statement of the Sages on "Torah and *gemilus chassadim*" does not appear in the above-quoted Talmudic text. This could be explained in the light of the following exposition, in sec. 3 of the *maamar* beginning *Ki Tishma BeKol,* in *Likkutei Torah:* "Our Sages taught that 'it would have been preferable....' This simply means that one should engage both in Torah study and in the practice of good deeds, and in fact in the practice of the *mitzvos* at large." Cf. also *Yevamos* 105a and *Tanya — Iggeres HaKodesh,* Epistle 5.
21. [Cf. *Megillah* 6b.]
22. [*Chagigah* 9b.]
23. See at length in the *maamar* beginning *Lech Lecha,* 5702.
24. [*Bereishis* 12:1.]

out from your land, your birthplace, and your father's home"; i.e., he was to depart from his material concerns and his habits. This is meant by "your birthplace" — his natural emotional traits. "Your father's house" refers to intellect, but more particularly, to the conceptions acquired through man's understanding, the approach to life which is called "a worldly perspective."

For example, this "worldly perspective" often distorts one's understanding of what is attractive and what is repulsive, referring to a repulsive quality as attractive and calling this, "manners." The reason for this behavior is that one accepts certain qualities which are not genuine, but rather superficial, intended only to impress another. Conversely, there are times when one labels something which is truly attractive as repulsive.

[This anomaly] stems from the fact that one follows his habits and natural tendencies which are physically and materially oriented. Therefore, the first step in a man's spiritual development is to shed these tendencies. It is through this that one becomes [a fit] receptor for the influence and revelation brought about by the Torah.

III

The concept can be explained as follows:[25] "The Holy One, blessed be He, desired to have a dwelling in the lower worlds." The Sages saw a hint to this in the verse,[26] "His thighs are pillars of marble based on sockets of fine gold."

"The word 'his thighs' [שוקיו in Hebrew] refers to this world which G-d desired [נשתוקק in Hebrew] to create. 'Pillars of marble' indicates that [the world] was created in six days [for the Hebrew שש means both 'marble' and 'six'].

---

25. [Cf. *Tanchuma, Parshas Bechukosai,* sec. 3.]
26. [*Shir HaShirim* 5:15.]

'Based on sockets of gold' refers to the portions of the Torah."[27]

On the verse,[28] "In the beginning G-d created...," our Sages note that the word בראשית ("in the beginning") comprises two elements — ב ראשית, implying "two firsts"; i.e., for the sake of two entities referred to as "first", the Jews and the Torah, G-d created the world.[29] This indicates that the ultimate intent of the creation of the world is that the Jews should study the Torah in the form in which it was given in this world. This fulfills [G-d's] intention in creating [all] the worlds, [i.e., the higher spiritual realms as well as this material world].

It is written,[30] "Torah is light." This implies that when all the aspects of existence are conducted according to the Torah, then the world will be maintained. Thus, our Sages declared,[31] "The Holy One, blessed be He, made a condition with all the works of Creation: If Israel accepts the Torah, you will continue to exist; if not, I shall return you all to nothingness and void.'"

Fulfilling the Torah means that the *mitzvos* are observed as prescribed by the Torah. The Hebrew מצוה ["commandment"] is related to the word צוותא, meaning "connection". [On a very basic level,] giving a command establishes a connection between the commander and the people who receive the commands. On the material plane, we see that a command is only relevant between people who share a connection, e.g., a father commands a son, or a master, his servant. Furthermore, the fulfillment of a command in general, and in particular, the commitment to fulfill it in a precise manner, indicates the depth of the con-

---

27. Cf. *Midrash Rabbah, ad loc.*
28. [*Bereishis* 1:1.]
29. [*Bereishis Rabbah* 1:6 and *Vayikra Rabbah* 36:4.]
30. [*Mishlei* 6:23.]
31. [*Shabbos* 88a.]

nection shared by the one receiving the command with the commander.

[To illustrate:] The way the commands of a master are fulfilled differs in several respects from the way the commands of a father are fulfilled. Sons possess an essential quality lacking in servants. Conversely, there is a superiority in the acceptance of the yoke [of servitude], which servants possess over sons. Both [sons and servants] share a common factor: It is through the fulfillment of a command that they, the recipients of the commands, establish their connection and bond with the commander.

[In a spiritual sense,] it is the fulfillment of the commandments which brings pleasure to the Creator. As our Sages teach,[32] "I derive satisfaction from the fact that I made a statement and My will was fulfilled."

The *mitzvos* represent G-d's will. Consequently, the primary element of service is that they be fulfilled with *kabbalas ol*, ["acceptance of the yoke of the Kingdom of Heaven"]. The fulfillment of G-d's will, i.e., the *mitzvos*, should not be motivated by an intellectual rationale, but rather by the realization that G-d's wisdom and His will decreed and commanded us [to fulfill them in a particular manner].

[From this perspective,] there is no difference between the different *mitzvos*. There are some *mitzvos* which mortal intellect accepts, e.g., honoring one's parents, charity, and the prohibitions against theft and robbery. There are other *mitzvos*, e.g., Pesach[33] and *tzitzis*,[34] which are defined as

---

32. *Sifri, Bamidbar* 28:8; and see also 15:7.
33. *Shmos* 13:10. The definition of Pesach as a *chok* follows the view of Rabbi Akiva (and, in *Mechilta deRashbi*, of Rabbi Eliezer).
34. The definition of *tzitzis* as a *chok* can be understood in the light of the analysis by the *Maharsha* (on *Yoma* 67b) of the rule enunciated by the Sages (cf. *Chullin* 109b): "Whatever the Torah forbade in one situation and

chukim, (*mitzvos* which transcend the intellect). [These differences only reflect one level and,] in essence, there is no difference whatsoever between *mitzvos*. Even those *mitzvos* that can be grasped intellectually ought to be fulfilled only because they are G-d's will.

The proper fulfillment of *mitzvos* depends on the study of Torah. On the most basic level, it is necessary to study in order to know how to fulfill the *mitzvos*. Indeed, we find a number of G-d-fearing individuals who lack basic knowledge: e.g., when it is permitted to interrupt one's prayers to respond *Amen* and *Amen, yehei shmei rabbah*; the laws of washing one's hands; and the careful observance of the *Shabbos* laws. These people ought to study in order to know how to fulfill the *mitzvos* according to the Torah.

Beyond this dimension, Torah study — and, in particular, communal Torah study — reveals a sublime light from above which arouses one to change his nature and habits, becoming a different person, and acquiring positive character traits.

IV

A person should meditate and realize that the ultimate purpose underlying the descent of his soul into his body is that he fulfill *mitzvos* and study Torah in this material world, [demonstrating that] this descent is for the sake of an eventual ascent. Through his spiritual labors in refining his animal soul and overcoming all hindrances and obstacles, his G-dly soul ascends, level beyond level. [He must also realize] that everything is dependent on himself.

When a person concentrates on these ideas, he will be motivated to approach the service of G-d and to establish fixed times for Torah study, [so that he can learn] how to

---

permitted in another is considered to be a *chok.*" The *Maharsha* here cites the seeming anomaly of *shaatnez* in *tzitzis*.

fulfill G-d's *mitzvos* with inner vitality. He will also carry out his resolve in actual practice.

When he does so, [he will benefit from] "the light of Torah," i.e., Divine light will illuminate all his affairs. [This is a reflection of the dimension of Torah which is a revelation] from above, but is brought about through his own service. In this as well, communal Torah study is superior to individual study, for communal study draws down a more elevated light.

This can be understood by a comparison to prayer. Even in regard to prayer, in which the worshiper elevates himself from below, there is a difference between the prayers of the individual and those of the community, as explained above. Throughout the entire year, the influence drawn down by communal prayer is of an entirely different [and superior] nature to the arousal from below. Surely, this difference applies likewise to Torah study, in which influence is drawn down *from above*. [Communal study is thus superior,] for it grants power to draw down Divine influence.

This concept can be explained by comparing prayer *(tefillah)* and blessing *(berachah)*. Each and every individual has the potential to pray. In contrast, blessings can only be given by one who has the power to bless; for example, Avraham, of whom it is said,[35] "And you shall be a blessing." *Rashi* interprets this to mean: "The blessings are given over to your hand. Previously, they were in My hand and I blessed Adam and Noach. Now, they are in your hand and you may bless whomever you desire."

Similarly, a *Kohen* conveys blessings because the *Kohanim* were given the power to do so.

The difference between the two can be explained as follows: Prayer represents a dynamic of elevation from a lower

---

35. *[Bereishis 12:2; see Rashi, ad loc.]*

level; i.e., the person stands below the influence which he seeks, prays for it, and begs to draw it down. This is implicit in the typical expression of request, "May it be Your will..." (*Yehi ratzon...*). [I.e., it is necessary that a new Divine Will come into existence to fulfill the person's request.] Such a request may be made by anyone.

In contrast, in regard to blessing, a drawing down of influence from above, the one giving the blessing must be above the influence. Otherwise, it would be impossible for him to draw it down. Thus, the *Kohanim* declare,[36] "May G-d bless you and protect you," thereby (in the words of the Sages)[37] "blessing one with children and wealth," with the intention that the children be raised with the proper direction in the study of Torah and the fear of G-d, and "protecting one from negative forces." The Priestly Blessing continues: "May G-d cause His countenance to shine upon you...." All this is recited as a command and a decree, [obligating G-d, as it were, to bestow these blessings,] because this is the nature of blessing, to draw down influence from above. Since the *Kohanim* were granted this potential from above, they have the power to draw down this influence.

A comparable potential [for a Jew to draw down G-dly light through Torah study] was granted at the time of the Giving of the Torah through the statement,[38] "And G-d spoke all these words, saying." [In the Torah, the word] "saying", *leimor*, [generally implies that a command should be conveyed to another individual. In this instance, however,] that was not necessary, for the entire Jewish people heard the Torah as given by G-d. Thus, [in this instance,] the Divine directive *"leimor"* grants each and every Jew of

---

36. [*Bamidbar* 6:24.]
37. [*Midrash Rabbah* and *Sifri, ad loc.*]
38. [*Bamidbar* 20:1.]

future generations the potential to draw down G-dliness through his Torah study.

[To emphasize every individual's ability to acquire the Torah,] the Torah was given in the desert.³⁹ [Our Sages explain, just as the desert is ownerless,] so, too, the crown of Torah was left free for every individual to acquire. Thus, every Jew has the potential to draw down the revelation of G-dliness when he studies Torah with the intent of fulfilling it, except that the community has been given greater potential than an individual.

This, then, is the meaning of the teaching: "When ten people sit and occupy themselves with Torah, the Divine Presence rests among them. (This is a reference to communal Torah study.)... From where do we learn that the same is true even of one? For it is said, 'In every place where I will have My Name mentioned, I will... bless you.'" [Although any study of the Torah draws down G-dly influence, communal study is more effective; hence the various levels mentioned in the *mishnah*.]

Of primary importance is studying Torah *with a colleague*. This is an act of spiritual *tzedakah*, which makes one's own mind and heart one thousand times more refined,⁴⁰ and arouses the Source of all blessings. This takes place because the thirteen principles of Biblical exegesis draw down the Thirteen Attributes of Divine Mercy and elicit blessings on the material plane — with visible and revealed good, in regard to one's children, health and livelihood. And may they all be granted in abundance.

---

39. [*Bamidbar Rabbah* 19:15.]
40. Cf. the *maamar* beginning *HaShamayim Kis'i* in *Torah Or*; the concept is explained in *Likkutei Torah LeGimmel Parshiyos* (*Toras Shmuel, Shaar Alef*).